GO TO YOUR ROOM!

CONSEQUENCES THAT TEACH

SHARI STEELSMITH

Raefield-
Roberts,
Publishers

D0291250

Acknowledgments

This book is a result of many parents' sharing of ideas—both ones that worked and ones that didn't. I am grateful to all who contributed ideas and stories which helped shape the book, particularly, Christi Hartman, Mimi Duffin, Denise Ainslie, Helen Neville, and Melody Young. Thank you to my editor, Gayle Bittinger, for her thoughtful work. Thanks also to the many parents and professionals who field-tested the manuscript and made it much better with their suggestions. Thanks, as always, to Betsy Crary and Karen Townsend for their professional perspectives and comments. Lastly, heartfelt thanks to my husband, Jim, for helping me carve out the time to write this book!

Dedicated to all my children: Catriel, Ben-Daniel, and Jonathan

Cover design and illustration by
Lightbourne, copyright © 2000

ISBN 0-9650477-2-5
Library of Congress Card Catalog number 99-75209

Co-Published by:
Raefield-Roberts, Publishers
25415 Bellview St.
Hemet, CA 92544

and

Parenting Press, Inc.
P.O. Box 75267
Seattle, WA 98125

CONTENTS

6 Planning for a Specific Problem 146

Other Good Books 153

Index 157

INTRODUCTION

The very genesis of this book began one day in the middle of my kitchen. My three-year-old son had just defiantly screamed "No!" in response to my telling him to put on his shoes. I leaned up against the sink, closed my eyes and thought, "I ought to have a good, logical consequence to give him that will help him learn not to scream at his mother—but all I can think of is how much *I* want to scream." Knowing I couldn't let his behavior go unchecked, I sent him to his room. But I wasn't happy with that consequence. It wasn't logically related to his offense, and I was pretty sure he didn't learn anything about how to behave better. I suspected (rightly so) that the behavior would reoccur. "I need a book that suggests good learning-oriented consequences," I thought, "one that will give me *lots* of ideas I can plan to use later when the misbehavior comes up."

You are holding that book in your hands. *Go to Your Room!* is the result of many parenting experts' recommendations for good consequences to use with children, and perhaps more importantly, the tried-and-true consequences parents have successfully used with their own children.

The book discusses the importance and use of con-sequences as a guidance tool; lists common misbehaviors in children ages 3-14 and several different, learning-oriented consequences for those behaviors; and also offers tips on delivering the consequences and following through. The reason there are more than one recommended consequence for any misbehavior is two-fold: no two children are exactly alike and no one child always responds in the same way. As a parent you need many different ideas and techniques to use with your children. The more ideas you have avail-able, the more likely you are to find something that works with your particular child.

Using logical consequences is only one tool in the parenting toolbox and should not be over-used. Parents who rely exclusively on consequences will find their effectiveness gradually wanes. Preventive techniques and generally good parenting skills will dramatically reduce the need for logical consequences in the first place. You will find references to other guidance methods or ways of avoiding the problems sprinkled throughout the book.

I encourage you to read thoughtfully through the book, keeping in mind your particular child with her unique temperament, and choose the consequences that will best help her learn.

1
YOUR RULES AND
WHEN YOUR CHILDREN
BREAK THEM

When discussing consequences, it is helpful to look at what your goals are after your child misbehaves. The real goals most parents hold for their children are to *learn* and to *change*. She needs to learn why her behavior is wrong and how it affects others and herself. This is especially true for younger children. Then she needs to change her behavior. Sometimes, however, children already understand a rule and choose to misbehave anyway.

In parenting my own children and after speaking with many, many parents, it is clear to me that parents' goals for children after misbehavior are for their children to:

Take responsibility for their actions. You want your children to "own up" to their wrongdoing—preferably voluntarily. You want them to answer honestly when you ask them if they have broken a rule. You do not want to hear them blaming others for their decisions and actions. You teach children to take responsibility by holding them accountable for their behavior. Holding children accountable is often accomplished by imposing consequences.

Have regret. This develops more and more with age as the child grows in empathy. I remember how horrified I was to see my two-year-old son whack his favorite little cousin on the head with a *rock* and then how appalled I was to find that he was not sorry about it at all! Parents teach their children to have regret for misdeeds by fostering empathy for others. Consequences are not the main teaching tool here, but they can help by imposing a certain amount of discomfort or inconvenience on the child. When the discomfort is logically related to the offense, the child is encouraged to have some regret for the action.

Make amends or repair the damage. This process is perhaps the most valuable in helping children achieve the above goals of taking responsibility and having regret. When a child willingly tries to right a wrong, he is taking responsibility for his actions, and he is usually face-to-face with the effects his misbehavior had on another. Making amends is a logical consequence itself. We will look at this more later.

The achievement of these goals is related to the child's overall cognitive development and to the specific development of morality. How able or willing the child is to work on them will depend on her age and understanding. Preschoolers are certainly able to begin learning about and practicing all three. Children younger than three can benefit by hearing their parents talk about these things, but don't expect them to fully understand or practice them.

Here are a few examples of ways to talk to toddlers and twos that promote responsibility, empathy, and making amends:

Responsibility:	"Uh oh. You broke the toy." "The rule is No throwing. You must mind the rule."
Empathy:	"No. Hitting hurts Mommy. Touch gently." "See how Sarah's face looks when she's sad?"
Making amends:	"Give Dalton a hug and tell him 'Sorry.'" "Help Brittany pick up the blocks you knocked down."

YOUR RULES AND WHY YOU HAVE THEM

The rules need to come first. The inevitable misbehavior ought to come second. If you do not have clear rules in your home, then you are not just failing to prevent problems, you are *inviting* limit-testing and misbehavior. Children will look for limits. If they don't find them, they will push harder and harder, looking for that wall. Parent educator and counselor John Rosemond writes, "Learning the distinction between acceptable and unacceptable behavior is the most difficult task of childhood and the most demanding of parenting. There are no options here—the child *must* learn and we *must* teach."[1]

Setting rules and enforcing them are two of the important ways parents show respect for children. It's a way of saying, "I care enough about you to correct you and teach you to do better." Children show respect for parents by adhering to those rules. When your rules are clear, the consequences for misbehavior will feel just, or fair, to the child. If there are no clear rules, he can say, "I didn't know I wasn't supposed to ...go to Bryan's house without asking ...stay out after 5pm, etc." Your consequences will then feel unfair to him, and he will spend his energy being mad at you instead of learning.

Your children need to know the reasons behind your rules. Don't assume they know because it seems obvious to you. It's surprising how many children can say what their parents *don't* want them to do, but they don't know why, and they can't tell you what their parents want them to do instead. I suggest you ask your children to tell you the reasons behind your rules. For example, you might say to your four year old, "No standing on counters. Use a stool to reach what you need." *(Help her down.)* "Tell me why we don't stand on the counters." The four year old might answer, "Because I could fall" or "I don't know." Reinforce the right answer or give the child the information she lacks: "That's right. Our rule is to be safe" or "Standing on counters is dangerous. You might fall and get hurt."

Parent educators Linda and Richard Eyre recommend parents teach their children to think of obedience in terms of observing rules and laws, not in terms of obeying people.[2] This is a useful concept. We want our children to respect adults, but not at the cost of our values and rules. Children carry our rules with them wherever they go. If your rule is

No snacks before dinner, then you want your child to follow that rule no matter where he is and who he is with.

HOW CONSEQUENCES IMPACT YOUR RULES

Consequences enforce your rules. It is helpful to have some general standing rules, that is, "house rules" with consequences children are aware of beforehand. Some common standing rules in families are:

> *Work before play.* Chores and homework come before any fun or discretionary activities.
>
> *Privilege goes with responsibility.* If a child shows a lack of responsibility, he loses the accompanying privileges.

The fun activities or privileges will vary from child to child. It is up to the parent to identify them and control the child's access to them, based on his adherence to the rules.

Your rules deserve respect. Your children show them respect by following them. You show the rules respect by enforcing them and by refusing to re-negotiate them on the spot (i.e., "Well, I guess it's okay just this one time"). Such off-hand re-negotiating disrespects your rules and invites further bargaining and begging the next time you try to deliver a consequence. Be fair and firm.

Let me note here that some children are only obedient to rules out of fear, not out of respect. If you frequently use physical discipline (ie., spanking) this may be the case. I will address physical discipline in Chapter 2. Strive for respect, not fear. You accomplish this by setting fair rules (appropriate to the child's age and development), making sure your children know the reasons behind the rules, and by consistently enforcing them.

Although I discourage re-negotiating rules during or just after misbehavior, it can be very appropriate to re-negotiate a rule in general. For example, as children grow older, their responsibilities and privileges change—and the rules need to reflect this. Changing a rule is best done when everyone is calm (*not* during a rule violation or when enforcing a consequence). I recommend using a family meeting to make such changes. We will discuss family meetings later.

In the next chapter we will go on to look at the consequences themselves.

1. John Rosemond, *Parent Power! A Common Sense Approach to Parenting in the 90's and Beyond,* 2nd ed., (Kansas City, MO: Andrews & McNeel, 1990), p.36.

2. Linda Eyre and Richard Eyre, *Teaching Children Values,* (New York: Simon & Schuster, 1993), p. 231.

2
WHAT ARE CONSEQUENCES?

There are two kinds of consequences used in parenting: natural and logical. Natural consequences happen without any parental intervention. If Benjamin forgets to bring his homework to school, he gets a failing grade on that assignment. If Ashley doesn't clean her room, she lives in a mess. If Eric fails to practice the piano, he must deal with his teacher's displeasure the next time he goes to a lesson.

Natural consequences are great teachers: they are always related to the offense, they happen automatically, and the child must deal with them. They teach the child about the natural and social order of the world.

When I was about seven years old, I received a new bike for Christmas. It was pastel-colored and had a white basket. I loved it. But I also took it for granted. After I rode it, I would carelessly leave it by the edge of the driveway instead of putting it away in the garage. My parents reminded me to put it away and warned me it could get stolen. Still, sometimes I did put it away and sometimes I didn't. One night the bike was stolen. I was crushed. My parents drove me around the greater neighborhood looking for the bike one weekend, but to no avail. A month or two later, they bought me an old, second-hand bike. It was big, three different colors, and ungainly. My brother called it the Jalopy. I didn't love this bike too much, but I took much better care of it.

☼

As a child I loved the great big, chocolate Easter eggs with sweet creme fillings and decorated lavishly with frosting flowers. My parents didn't buy this sort of thing at Easter, so I was delighted when my great-uncle Vic gave me such an egg one year. I decided that it was too beautiful to eat and I would keep it on my dresser forever. The very next morning I woke to find a huge, gaping hole in my chocolate egg with kitten prints in the filling. Jericho, my kitten, had a feast in the night. Horrified, I carried the egg and tale to my mother. She listened sympathetically—and she did not offer to buy me another egg.

The above two natural consequences were very effective teachers for me. I learned (the hard way) what happens if you don't take care of your possessions. My parents wisely did not rescue me from my choices; they did not buy another new bike, and they did not replace the Easter egg.

WHEN NATURAL CONSEQUENCES DON'T WORK

When natural consequences fail to change a child's behavior, it is usually because the consequence doesn't matter to the child—maybe Ashley doesn't mind a messy room or Benjamin is not particularly disturbed to receive a bad grade. In this case, parents need to impose a logical consequence that has more meaning or impact on the child, or use a different parenting tool altogether.

Beware of sabotaging natural consequences. Many parents deem natural consequences unreasonable or too harsh and "rescue" their children from them. This is illustrated in the parent who continually brings the forgotten lunch to school, who pays the speeding ticket for the teen, or who constantly reminds a child to do a necessary chore. Author and educator Jane Nelson writes, "Children will never learn to be responsible for their own behavior as long as adults take that responsibility away from them by repeating reminders or by solving problems *for* them rather than *with* them."[1]

Let natural consequences teach without further embellishment or lectures from you. Restrain yourself from saying, "I told you it was cold and you needed to keep your mittens on. Now look how blue your hands are. Does that feel good?" Scolding or lecturing diminishes the learning that comes with natural consequences.

Natural consequences are often a sufficient response to a misdeed. The child learns without the parent's involvement. Sometimes, however, when family rules are broken, a parent needs to act in addition to a natural consequence —especially if a logical consequence is set up in advance. The rule in Sam's family is you do not take the family car without permission or you lose your driving privileges. Sam took the car without asking and went to the library. He broke the speed limit on the way and received a ticket for $100.00. The natural consequence for speeding was expensive and Sam was horrified. Although his parents felt the ticket was punishment enough, they still withdrew his driving privileges for a week in order to honor the family rule. Sam was also required to pay for the ticket from his own money. The teens in this family learned a valuable lesson about actions and consequences and whether their parents would follow-through on their rules.

Some natural consequences are so intense that parents will need to support their child through the experience. Perhaps a child loses her best friend by betraying a confidence. In this case, a hug is an appropriate response with a reassuring comment like, "It's a hard lesson to learn. I know you'll have another best friend someday and you will be careful of confidences." Remember, your goal for your child is learning, not suffering or humiliation.

Natural consequences are not appropriate at the following times: when a child is in danger (you can't let your child experience the natural consequence of diving into a shallow pool), when another person would be hurt or inconvenienced (for example, letting your child throw bricks at someone), or if the child does not care about the consequence—and many children are perfectly willing to experience slight natural consequences to get what they want. Use logical consequences or other guidance methods to deal with these times.

WHAT ARE LOGICAL CONSEQUENCES?

Logical consequences are imposed by adults, related to the offense, and help the child learn. Many people use the terms logical consequence and punishment interchangeably. There are, however, differences between the two.

Logical Consequences: *Vs.*	*Punishments:*
▪ Help the child change behavior through learning	▪ Change child's behavior through suffering/deprivation
▪ Are delivered calmly and objectively	▪ Are delivered emotionally/ angrily
▪ Are consistent with nurturing care	▪ Can involve pain or humiliation

- Feel fair to the child
- Relate logically to mis-behavior

- Feel unfair to the child
- May result in child feeling vengeful, rebellious, or secretive ("next time I won't get caught")

Punishment is usually very effective in stopping mis-behavior at the time. It is much less effective in accom-plishing a long-term behavior change. If you are like most parents, you usually set consequences and occasionally punish without thinking much about it. Your logical con-sequences may not work because they are impulsively or casually-chosen. My goal in this book is to get you to think about the process of setting consequences very deliberately, plan your responses to misbehavior ahead of time, and by so doing, avoid punishing. After all, how much of your time do you really want to spend being angry, yelling, and punishing? Wouldn't you rather be calm, deliberate, and get lasting results? Logical consequences can help you do this.

EXAMPLES OF LOGICAL CONSEQUENCES

You set a logical consequence for a child when no natural ones occur, or if the natural consequences don't bother the child. Some simple examples are below.

Six-year-old Amy throws her dirty clothes on the floor instead of in the hamper. Her mother said for every time she found dirty laundry on the floor, she would remove one favorite shirt for a week. Amy loved her Barbie™ T-shirts and was very upset to lose three of them the first week. She began to put her dirty clothes in the hamper.

The above logical consequence was a good one because:

- It was related to the offense (when Amy was irresponsible with her clothes, she lost a favorite article of clothing).
- It was enforceable (Mother was the laundry person in the home and was in a position to enforce the rule).
- It was reasonable (the consequence was fair and proportional to the misdeed).
- It was calmly delivered by the parent (Mother didn't yell and complain each time she found dirty clothes on the floor, she just quietly removed a shirt from Amy's drawer).
- It helped Amy learn that privileges (wearing Barbie™ shirts) are contingent upon responsibility (taking care of dirty clothes).

Here is an example from my own family.

For the umpteenth time I reminded my nine-year-old stepson that beds are not for jumping on. The next time it happened, I told him that since he had so much wild energy he could use it up by running around the outside of the house five times. He grinned at me and began running laps. He didn't make it five times, but he did come back with much less restless energy.

This consequence was effective because:

- It was related to the offense (it redirected his physical energy into a more appropriate arena).
- It was reasonable (the consequence was proportional to the offense—and after a good-faith effort and his energy was spent, I didn't insist he finish all five laps).
- It was delivered calmly by the parent (I managed to be matter-of-fact about it instead of overly irritated).
- It helped my stepson learn that when he is full of

physical energy, there are better places to spend it than on the furniture.

When my son was three, he was very impressed by a dramatic neighbor lady who frequently said "Oh my God!" in everyday conversation. My son began mimicking her and repeating this phrase four or five times a day. Each time I would correct him and explain that, in our family, we don't say that. It didn't help. I thought about the problem and decided on a plan. The next time he said it, I took him into his room and put his church clothes on. When he questioned me, I said, "Well, since you want to talk about God so much, I thought we'd just get your church clothes on and take you to church so you can learn to talk about God respectfully." He was horrified and promised never to use the phrase again. It solved the problem.

This consequence was successful because:

- It was related (church clothes and the prospect of a mid-week trip to church helped my son connect with the concept of using God's name reverently no matter where he was).
- It was reasonable and proportional to the offense.
- It was appropriate to my son's developmental level and temperament (this might not work with an older child or a child who loves to sit still).
- It was enforceable (I was the one usually around when the phrase came out).
- It was delivered calmly (I was matter-of-fact in my tone of voice, not angry or irritated, so my son experienced the consequence as logical instead of punishing).

I can't say that all my consequences are creative and successful. But I can say that the ones I put some time and thought into are generally the most effective. If I've thought about a consequence ahead of time, I'm prepared the next time the misbehavior comes up. And it always does! It also helps to discuss your child's recurrent misbehavior and brainstorm ideas for consequences with your partner. Decide on a plan of action together. Then whoever is on duty the next time the misbehavior occurs is prepared.

WARNINGS: SHOULD YOU USE THEM?

In general, I find warnings in the form of a choice most useful. Such a choice is not a consequence itself, but serves as a warning that one is lurking in the wings. For example, you might say, "You can choose to eat your green beans or you can choose to go without dessert" or "You can finish your homework now or you can do the dishes for me and then finish your homework." The choice functions as a reminder or a warning that the power for choosing either good behavior or an undesirable consequence lies solely in the child's hands. *She* has the power to make her life comfortable or uncomfortable. There is no pay-off here for defiance.

A simple warning sounds like, "Don't do that anymore or I will...." The slight, but important difference here is that the emphasis is on your power; you will decide and deliver the consequence if the child refuses to comply. It is less obvious that the child has a choice in the situation. You have more chance of gaining cooperation from your child if you frame the warning as a choice.

Only offer the choice or give a warning *once*. If the child continues the misbehavior, then he has made his choice. Honor that choice by imposing the consequence immediately. Parents who do not follow through by giving the consequence teach their children to ignore them.

SHOULD CHILDREN HELP SET CONSEQUENCES?

I think it is very useful to get your children's input on logical consequences for violations of the family rules. Be aware that children will often choose or suggest much harsher consequences than parents do; be prepared to adjust any consequences that need it.

Discussing family rules and setting standing consequences is a great opportunity for a family meeting. Attendance is mandatory, even for the smallest family members. In our family, we sit around the dining room table and start with each person saying what he or she loves about each family member. For example, we might pick my husband first and go around the table, round-robin style, each saying one thing we love about Daddy. We do this for every family member. It sets a positive, caring mood. We then discuss whatever problem we're working on, brainstorm solutions (no criticisms allowed during brainstorming), and collectively decide on what we'll try first. Then we eat some kind of fun dessert.

Having children know consequences in advance is very useful—it can act as a deterrent to a misbehavior and you get less protesting and arguing when you enforce the consequence. Knowing the consequence in advance is not, however, always necessary or practical. You cannot always predict the misbehaviors that your children will indulge in (children are creative!) and so you cannot always establish an appropriate consequence in advance.

WHEN ARE LOGICAL CONSEQUENCES NEEDED?

I suggest using logical consequences when the misbehavior occurs repeatedly and your best efforts with other parenting tools have not worked. If you are at your wit's end with a child's behavior and are inclined to respond emotionally, then that's a cue for you to give yourself a time-out and do some thinking. There are plenty of ways to deal with the problem you probably haven't even tried yet. Chances are you have been using the same response over and over again and you are frustrated that the child isn't responding. Try talking with your partner, or a friend about the problem and brainstorm three things to try. Use logical consequences last. I have generally found our home a happier place when I limit my reliance on logical consequences and exhaust my other options first.

AVOIDING SITUATIONS THAT REQUIRE CONSEQUENCES

There are so many parenting tools that will solve behavior problems, it makes sense to try them before you resort to consequences. The following are a few examples of parenting techniques that *avoided* a consequence scenario.

Thirteen-year-old John was on the junior high football team. During fund-raising, he was given the task of selling candy bars door-to-door. For one solid week, the box of candy stayed on his bedroom floor, untouched. His mother grew anxious and reminded him several times to get out and sell the candy. Then she overheard him on the phone with his coach, fibbing about the amount of candy he'd sold. Mother felt angry, since she'd reminded him plenty of times to sell the candy and angrier still about the lie he'd told. Then she decided to step back and discuss the matter with his father that night. Dad brought up a good point: did John know how to sell things door-to-door? Upon reflection, Mother admitted that he had only sold things to family members in previous "sales" experiences. Dad committed to spending some time with John that weekend to teaching the necessary skills and providing moral support by going along on the sales venture.

Parenting technique used: Teaching skills

Devon (age 3) and Sarah (age 3) were playing with action figures. Devon wanted to use both of the blue Batmans™. Sarah wanted a blue Batman™ too. They began quarreling. "You can figure out a way to share the Batmans or I can put them away for the afternoon," said Dad. Devon and Sarah looked at each other in alarm. "How about if you use the pink Power Ranger™?" Devon offered. "Okay," said Sarah, "and the other Batman™ can be their little boy."

Parenting technique used: Give a choice.

✿

Seven-year-old Katie was not a morning person. She had a hard time rolling out of bed in the morning and accomplishing all of her morning tasks. Every morning her mother would nag at her to hurry up or to not forget something. Mom was tired of being responsible for Katie making the bus on time and was annoyed when she left for school without making her bed or brushing her hair. Katie was grouchy when Mom nagged her.

They sat down one night and discussed their morning routine. Mom suggested establishing a sequence of events that Katie had to do in the same order each morning so she wouldn't forget anything: make bed, get dressed, brush teeth and hair, eat breakfast, gather school things, and be out the door by eight in the morning to catch the bus. Katie agreed to the plan. They made a chart and posted it on the back of Katie's door. After a week of following the new routine, Katie's morning performance improved dramatically and Mom was out of the loop.

Parenting technique used: Create a routine

✿

Dad was frustrated that his children were not doing their chores before dinner. Adam (age 12), Kayla (age 10), and Aaron (age 6) would watch TV when they came home from school and leave all their chores and homework for the evening. Then there would be a lot of rushing and irritation after dinner and not everything got done.

Dad called a family meeting. He served berry cobbler and then brought up the problem, "I'm upset with the way our evenings are. You kids are leaving too much to do after dinner. Then you are rushed and don't do a good job on either homework or chores. Sometimes you get to bed way too late and lose sleep. What can we do about this problem?" A discussion ensued and the children came up with several ideas including: have Dad help with the dishes; a new rule that you must do all your chores before dinner; save all the chores for the weekend; only watch one hour of TV a day and tape the TV shows they want to watch and only view them after all chores or homework are done. Dad vetoed a few options and then they took a vote. They decided to do all their chores before dinner and tape any special shows they want to watch. They would do homework after dinner.

Parenting technique used: Family meeting and problem solving

The parents in the above examples could have used consequences at the outset of the problem solving process, but they may have been less effective and there probably would not have been as much cooperation from their children. If these methods had not worked, the parents in the above examples could have tried another guidance method and then resorted to consequences.

REWARDS AND CONSEQUENCES: TWO SIDES OF THE SAME COIN

Rewards are a good parenting tool for many situations. They are very similar to consequences in this way:

Reward = desirable consequence for good behavior.
Logical consequence = undesirable consequence for
misbehavior.

Rewards, used correctly, are not bribes. Parents bribe their
children when they dangle something in front of them to
stop or prevent misbehavior, for example, saying to the child
in the grocery cart, "If you stop screaming, I'll buy you a
candy bar." In this scenario, the parent is desperate and the
child knows it. The child may even learn to scream to get
candy.

A reward is a motivator for good behavior in the first
place. Rewards are properly given *after* the good behavior
or finished task. For example, the parent who says in the
car, "I expect pleasant voices in the grocery store and
everyone to stay next to the cart. Each child who does this
may choose a treat in the candy aisle." If the parent stays
calm and follows through with his plan, rewarding those
who choose to cooperate and matter-of-factly withholding
treats from those who don't, then he has successfully used
a reward system.

Rewards make a great deal of sense to me. Do I want
to motivate my child using a positive consequence for good
behavior, or do I want to motivate him to behave by using
a logical consequence for bad behavior? I'd like to use
positive consequences whenever possible, so I try to "catch
my kids being good" and reward them accordingly. I don't,
however, use rewards on an everyday basis. I have found
them most useful when my children are working on a big
task.

My son is not very happy in the water. As an infant, it
took him a full year to feel safe and enjoy his bath. Since we
live in southern California, my husband and I felt it im-

perative that he be pool-safe as soon as possible. He had swimming lessons during his two- and three-year-old summers and made minimal progress. This past summer he began swimming lessons with his usual massive fussing. There would be worrying and crying ahead of time, and wailing during the lesson. Our value on safety overrode his discomfort, and we kept him in the class.

At the second lesson I noticed that although he fussed horribly at the teacher, he still cooperated with all her requests: putting his face in the water, kicking, and dog-paddling. I suspected that he just needed a little help with controlling his emotions.

That night my husband took him to the local toy store and told him he could pick out any toy he wanted. He would buy the toy and put it on top of the refrigerator at home. My son would not be allowed to touch it until he completed one fuss-free swim lesson. He eagerly selected a supremely-ugly bug toy, and they brought it home.

I found him gazing at the unreachable toy several times. He began controlling himself halfway through the next lesson. The day after that he earned the toy. His swim lessons became much more productive. He just needed the little extra motivation of a reward to help him turn the corner.

Children respond well to rewards if it is something they truly want, if they receive the reward (or a portion of it) promptly, and if rewards are not over-used. My cousin uses a variety of parenting techniques, including both reward systems and consequences, with her four children. After one particularly trying evening, she responded to some backtalk by giving her eleven-year-old son an extra chore. He gave her a funny look and went off to do the dishes. Ten minutes later he reappeared and said, "Mom, I like it better when you give us good stuff *[rewards]*, instead of bad stuff *[consequences]*." I think most children would agree.

CONSEQUENCES WILL NOT SUCCEED ALONE

Make no mistake about it. I believe in using well-chosen consequences that inspire learning. I also believe that a daily diet of consequences will produce resentful and discouraged children. We all need positive strokes. Educator and author Jean Illsley Clarke points out that we need two different kinds: strokes for "being" and strokes for "doing."[2]

Affirmations for Being

We all need to know that we are valuable to our families. You give your child positive messages for "being" by saying things like, "I'm glad you're my daughter" or "I love you" or "You're such a great kid." You can do this non-verbally with a hug, smoothing your child's hair, rubbing his back, or blowing a kiss. I often hug my kids and say wonderingly, "I can't believe I was so lucky to get *you* as my children." You can give affirmations for being by sending a note in your child's lunch that says, "I miss you—have a great day!" or "Remember, I love you."

Daily departures and reunions are a great time to give and receive affirmations for being. My husband's favorite time of day is coming in the door at night and being hit by two hurtling rockets of affection. He often says, "I sure missed you" or "I love you *so* much." Affirmations for being are wonderful bits of proof that we are valuable and loved.

Affirmations for Doing

We also need positive strokes for what we do well and our efforts toward accomplishing goals. Affirmations for doing sound like this: "Great job making your bed" or "Wow, a B on the spelling test. Now that's improvement!"

or "I liked seeing how you shared your colored pencils with your sister—that was nice of you" or "You are such a good listener" or "Great game—I'll bet you're proud of that touchdown."

You have opportunities for giving these affirmations every day. No child messes up 24 hours a day—there is always something good to say if you take the time to notice and comment. As with affirmations for being, you can give affirmations for doing verbally or in writing, or by letting your child overhear you talk with someone else.

Affirmations for doing assure your child that you notice her strengths, efforts, and achievements as much or more than you do her shortcomings. This is no small thing.

Positive Reinforcers

Each of these positive reinforcers for good behavior motivate children to continue behaving well.

Attention—This can be verbal, as in the affirmations described above. It can be paying attention, like watching or listening, or it can be physical, like a hug. Take note, however, if a child cannot get your attention by being good, she may just get it by behaving badly. You don't really get to choose *whether* you give your children attention, you only get to choose how.

Praise—Affirmations for doing are praise. Praise needs to be sincere (no grandiose compliments like, "This is the best picture in the world!"), it needs to be immediate, and it needs to be specific. For example, when Cami brings home her weekly behavior report from school, her Dad could say, "Terrific, Cami. This shows real improvement in paying attention and finishing work. I'm proud of you." Dad is sincere (Cami is improving, not perfect), he gives the praise as soon as he receives the report, and he is specific about what she did well (simply saying "Good job, Cami" would not be specific).

Recognition—You recognize a child when you comment on a helpful action, praise an achievement, or just thank him for being himself. Hanging and displaying a child's artwork is recognition. Attending their sporting events, concerts, plays, or awards ceremonies recognizes their efforts and accomplishments. You can also have family celebrations to honor a child for achievements or milestones. In my family, we have started the tradition of a book-shaped cake to honor a new reader. Learning to swim gets my children a special Dad-designed certificate that is framed and hung in their room.

Rewards—Rewards are helpful when a child is trying to learn a new skill, learning to be responsible for a task, or working on achieving a goal. Rewards can help children learn faster and then be gradually phased out as the child becomes more competent in the skill. Many parents use stickers, pennies, or favorite treats as everyday rewards. I prefer to use a more expensive item and reserve it for a really big skill, like learning to swim. Whatever the reward is, it has to be something the child *really* wants. Also, be aware that a child will become satiated with the same reward after a while. I would caution parents to use material rewards sparingly. Any parenting method can become overused and therefore less effective. Rewards are no different from consequences in this respect.

If you want to make good use of consequences, you will be wise to use these positive reinforcers as well.

CONSEQUENCES TO AVOID

Back to consequences—this time the ones to avoid. No topic gets parents more stirred up, or uncomfortable, than whether or not they should spank their kids. Although I suspect there are very few parents out there who have never momentarily lost control and swatted their children, it is not a discipline tool I recommend. This is why.

Research shows regular spanking has harmful side effects. The Family Research Laboratory out of the University of New Hampshire has done studies[3] showing that children who are regularly spanked grow up four times more likely to be highly aggressive, two-and-a-half times more likely to hit a spouse, and are highly likely to spank their own children. There is also a high rate of depression among adults who were frequently spanked as children. For children who were spanked only occasionally, the rates of violence and depression are lower, but still more elevated than normal.

It stops misbehavior short-term, but does not elicit true obedience or responsibility. Spanking usually stops bad behavior in its tracks—but only for a short time. Instead of focusing on learning, the child usually spends her time resenting or fearing the parent and makes sure that the next time she misbehaves it's behind the parent's back. Spanking teaches children that you are required to behave only when someone more powerful is around to force you to. And remember this: when a child is scared—and being spanked is scary—no learning takes place.

It works best at relieving a parent's anger and frustration. Spanking works great at venting your own emotions. But is that really what you want to use your child for? If you're not willing, as a parent, to control your own emotions, then how can you expect your child to do so? Not many parents I know can truthfully say that they are calm and dispassionate when they spank their children. And after they spank, they usually feel some guilt.

It damages the parent-child bond. Children who are spanked regularly can begin to fear their parents. Now, there's nothing the matter with a little healthy respect, but a child who fears his parents is not going to come to them with legitimate worries and concerns. I have a friend who was spanked frequently as a child. He was also told that if he ever got into trouble at school, he could expect worse treatment at home. He was wrongfully accused of a misdeed at school, but refused to tell his parents about it for fear of being spanked.

One of my own less-than-stellar moments as a parent took place when my son was three years old. I was running his bath and leaning over the tub to adjust the water temperature. My hair brushed against his bare arm. He reached over and took a mouthful of my hair and pulled it out at the roots. I screamed and swatted him, hard. "Why did you do that?" I demanded, my eyes tearing up, "That hurt me!" His eyes got huge and he said quaveringly, "Sorry, Mommy" and burst into tears. I hugged him for a moment and said, "Never, never do that again." He pushed back from me and a look of astonishment came over his face, "Hey!" he said accusingly, "You hit me!" All regret and any learning that might have taken place vanished from his mind as he focused on the fact that I hit him. I heard about it constantly for a few days after that.

Although hitting my son got him to stop biting my hair, the hitting became the only relevant part of the story in his mind. His resentment with my punishment was what endured, not the importance of being gentle with others. The incident served to remind me that spanking does not mesh with my parenting goals.

Along with spanking, do your best to exclude from your discipline: hitting of all forms, pushing, kicking, pinching, out-of-control yelling, sarcasm of any kind, and deprivation (locking a child in a closet, taking away more than one meal, disallowing a child use of the bathroom, etc.) Any of these practices can easily cross the line and become abusive. Try to avoid them altogether.

THE NEXT STEP

Now that you know what consequences are, how they work, and which ones to avoid, we will move on to how to choose just the right one for your child.

1. Jane Nelson, Ed.D., *Positive Discipline,* rev. ed., (New York: Ballantine Books, 1996), p.97.

2. See *Self-Esteem: A Family Affair,* by Jean Illsley-Clarke, (New York: Harper & Row, 1978).

3. Murray A. Straus, *Ten Myths About Spanking Children,* (Durham, NH: Family Research Laboratory, University of New Hampshire, 1992).

3
CHOOSING AND USING THE RIGHT CONSEQUENCE FOR YOUR CHILD

I stated in the last chapter that a good consequence must be logically related to the offense. Natural consequences are automatically related and that's partially why they are effective. Too often, however, the consequences parents choose are not even remotely related to the misdeed. This doesn't mean the consequence automatically fails, but it won't necessarily feel fair to the child and it moves closer to being a punishment. If the child feels unjustly treated or punished, then a true change in heart and behavior is less likely.

When a consequence is related to the misdeed, it becomes more effective. Children can understand the logic behind it, and that's where the feeling of fairness (even though I guarantee you they still won't like it) comes from.

Alexis (age 3) had a lot of natural aggression. Although her parents were pleased that this temperament meant she would not become a "doormat" in her life, they were concerned that she resorted to hitting her playmates any time a conflict arose. They settled on a standing rule and consequence: if you mistreat a playmate, you lose the privilege of playing with people. When she hauled off and whacked her friends, Mom and Dad would send Alexis to her room, and, if possible, terminate the playdate. An only child, Alexis loved having friends over, so this consequence mattered a great deal to her.

This consequence is logical and related: if you hit people, you lose the privilege of being with them.

✡

John is concerned about his eight-and ten-year-old children telling lies. If he catches them in a fib, he then refuses to believe anything they say for the rest of the day. "It makes them furious," he says, "but it really makes an impression on them that telling the truth is important."

This consequence is logical and related: if you lie, you lose the right to be believed. It also helps children learn about the fragility of trust.

✡

Justin (age 10) is famous for losing his coats. His mother says it's not uncommon for him to lose three a year. Unhappy with his irresponsibility, she told him, "If you lose your coat, you will have to replace it with your own money. If you don't have enough money to pay for one, you will work off the debt in extra chores." Sure enough, Justin lost his coat. The next day his mother took him to the local discount store and he purchased an inexpensive, not so "cool" coat with his own money. Justin was not happy to wear the new coat, but he didn't lose it.

The consequence is logical and related: if you lose your coat, you pay for a new one.

A Quick Word About Toddlers and Two's

The younger set does so many unpredictable things, it's hard to come up with a truly logical consequence for each misbehavior. Try to focus on the problem areas that come up over and over again. For example, if your two year old has a tendency to hit a lot, choose a related consequence and follow through consistently—tell her to touch gently and then remove her from others' presence for a short time. Choosing a related consequence becomes much more important and relevant as children grow; three and certainly four year olds can make this connection more easily.

With some misdeeds, it can be very difficult to find a consequence that is related. Sometimes you know a certain logical consequence won't matter to the child—even if it is related and deserved. Later in this chapter I will talk more about matching the consequence to the child. Most of the time, however, if you give the matter enough thought, you can come up with a related consequence. The key here is not to grab something—anything—out of the air on the spot. If necessary, tell your child you're taking a time-out and that you'll get back to him on the consequences of his behavior. Don't take more than a day to decide for school-aged children. Preschool-aged children need to have the consequence much more quickly or they will forget what it is for. Toddlers need to experience simple consequences immediately after the misbehavior.

You can avoid impulsive choosing by keeping track of misbehavior and noticing when one problem keeps recurring. Then do some thinking on that problem and come up with a plan. Be prepared for the next time the misbehavior arises.

When you set family rules and choose consequences with your children, then you are in good shape. Everyone knows the rules and the consequences ahead of time. You don't have to do the thinking on the spot. You just need to calmly carry out the consequence.

"GROUNDED TILL NEXT CHRISTMAS?"

Logical consequences should be proportional in severity to the offense and reasonable for the age of the child. If your seven-year-old daughter fails to shut the door for the fifth time that day, taking away outside privileges for the whole week is excessive. If you tend to give severe consequences, then you are reacting emotionally, not dispassionately. Remember, consequences are for learning. If your daughter is inside for the entire week, she doesn't have much chance to practice remembering to shut the front door.

Parent educators pretty much agree on keeping a consequence short in duration. A philosophy of "Tomorrow is another day and another chance to try again" is a positive, optimistic position to take with your children. You want them to feel like you have faith in them to learn and do better.

Don't choose devastating consequences like cancelling a child's birthday party, taking away a long-worked-for treat or trip, or taking away a young child's "lovey." Consequences like time-out or grounding can seem mild to you in comparison to whatever the offense was, but a child does not have to *suffer* to learn.

In a similar vein, don't threaten to take away things like Christmas presents in order to scare or intimidate a child into obedience. It amounts to little more than a bribe. Parents who use these threats usually have no intention of following up on them, and the children eventually learn this and disregard the parent.

THE CONSEQUENCE MUST MATCH THE CHILD

I've pointed out earlier that a consequence won't work to change a child's behavior if the consequence doesn't matter to her. This is true of both natural and logical consequences. Not only must the consequence be reasonable, proportional to the offense, and appropriate to the child's age, it also must be compatible with the child's temperament and interests.

Kelli, age 17, had a habit of violating her 11pm curfew on weekends. She always seemed to have a reason why she couldn't make it in by 11pm—the movie went 15 minutes over, the driver wanted to stop for milkshakes, etc. Her mother was in the habit of grounding her for the next day if she broke her curfew. The consequence, although related, didn't bother her too much. In fact, her mother suspected she was deliberately casual about her curfew on nights when she had no special plans for the next day. After some thought, her mother revised the consequence. The next morning after Kelli broke her curfew, Mother said, "When you don't come home on time, I get worried, and I lose sleep. Because I lost sleep last night you will be responsible for my chores today so that I can rest." Mother handed a disbelieving Kelli a list of extra chores for her to do. The curfew problem soon disappeared.

This consequence worked much better because Kelli minded the extra chores more than she did being grounded. Here's another example of a consequence matching a particular child.

Kathryn, age 12, argued frequently with her parents. They didn't mind that so much, but really disliked the way she would get angry, run to her room, and slam the door while they were talking with her. Mom and Dad conferred about the problem. The next door slamming incident happened one morning before school. When Kathryn came home, she found her door had been removed from its hinges. Her parents told her, "If you abuse your door, you lose the right to have one. It is taking a well-deserved break for two days. You can have it back at the end of that time if there is no further door-slamming. You can dress in the bathroom until you've earned it back." Kathryn was furious, but began to control her door-slamming impulses.

Because her parents knew that privacy was important to Kathryn and made a very limited use of it in the consequence, it worked to change her behavior. Note that they were restrained in the amount of time the door spent off its hinges—the point was adequately made in a small amount of time and they demonstrated faith in her ability to earn it back and retain the privilege. If they had removed the door longer, or permanently, the consequence would quickly become a harsh punishment and only elicit resentment in Kathryn.

Lisa's eight-year-old son, Steven, was a sore loser. He would get very upset if his team lost and refuse to go shake hands with opponents after the game, or do so only grudgingly. At home, he would throw tantrums when he lost board games with his siblings. After watching several "poor loser" behaviors, Lisa came up with the following plan. The next time he wanted to play a game, she said, "You know Steven, I've noticed that you get very, very upset when you don't win a game. It really hurts me to see you feeling so badly, so I guess you'll have to sit out today so I don't get too hurt watching you." Steven objected and promised he would not get upset if he lost. "Well, I'm willing to give it a try," said Lisa, "but if you don't control your behavior, we'll have to cut off all sports and games (including games on TV, computer games, and Nintendo™ games) for two days."

Lisa knew Steven would need practice at controlling his feelings and expected some failures. During the next few weeks, Lisa watched TV sports with Steven and pointed out how professional athletes did or did not behave with good sportsmanship. They discussed how sore losers are usually worried about how losing makes them look, but in reality they look much, much worse by losing badly. It took about a month of consistently applying the consequence and having talks, but gradually Steven learned to control his behavior.

Lisa's consequence plan was effective because sports and games mattered so much to her son. He was motivated to change his behavior in order to be able to play.

Alec (age 5) loved chocolate brownies. He was not so fond, however, of eating his dinner and would complain about the vegetables and meat on his plate. His parents set a family rule. If you're not hungry enough to eat your dinner, you're not hungry enough for dessert. Alec only had to miss brownies once to begin making a good effort toward eating his dinner.

This consequence worked with Alec because he dearly loved desserts. It would not have worked with his little brother, Harrison, who was not so fond of sweets.

My friend's six-year-old daughter adores after-school snacks. My cousin's eight-year-old son lives for his Nintendo™ game time in the afternoon. These are prime privileges for removal. Only you know what matters to your child. The challenge is figuring out how to relate the removal of the privilege to the misbehavior. Make a list of his or her very favorite things to do. See if any of them are or can be related to a current problem.

COMMONLY-USED CONSEQUENCES

From my research with parents I've compiled a list of logical consequences that are frequently used. Sometimes seeing a list like the following can act as a catalyst for some creative thinking on picking a consequence for your own child.

Many of these consequences can be classified under the "Removal of Privileges" category. Choose only consequences you are absolutely sure you can follow through on. Remember, the consequence is for your child, not to punish you. Don't take away play time at the park if you are desperate to get the kids out of the house and have a breather.

Consequences for Ages 3-6

Time-out (one minute for each year of age)
Send child to room
Withhold playdate
20 minute earlier bedtime
20 minute time-out for toy
Come inside from play for 10 minutes
10 minute loss of play with friend or sibling
Loss of planned outing (park, walk) after one warning
10 minute loss of TV/computer/video game use
Loss of snack
20 minute restriction from pets

Consequences for Ages 6-10

Loss of radio/cd player for 15 minutes
30 minute earlier bedtime
30 minute loss of toy/game
Loss of outside play time
10-15 minute loss of play with sibling or friend

Loss of phone use for the afternoon/evening
Loss of planned outing (park, mall, movie) after one
  warning (but not special events, like parties)
Loss of bike/skateboard/skates for one afternoon
15-30 minute loss of TV/computer/video game use
Time-out (one minute for each year of age)
Loss of friend/playdate for the afternoon
Loss of sports, music, dance practice for the afternoon*
Loss of treat or dessert
20-30 minute restriction from pets

Consequences for Ages 11 and up

Loss of use of bedroom for limited time (no more than 1-2
  days)
Loss of one meal
Loss of household services, like laundry
Loss of TV viewing
Loss of computer use
Loss of phone use
Curfew restrictions
Loss of driving privileges
Loss of cheerleading/dance/sports practices
Loss of time with friends

---

*When you take away sports (or performance arts, like dance or music) activities, keep in mind that showing up for practices, rehearsals, games, or performances is an obligation your child has to the rest of the group. Talk to the coach or instructor before you take away practices or events; it's likely he will have a policy about how many practices the child can miss before being penalized. It's also probable that he will encourage your child to clean up his act at home in order to keep him participating.

Loss of eating-out privileges
Grounding* for the afternoon or one day

MAKING AMENDS AS A CONSEQUENCE

I mentioned using restitution, or making amends, as a consequence earlier in this book. This is particularly appropriate when a child's misbehavior has infringed on the rights of another. Educator and author Jean Illsley Clarke points out that consequences that teach do not necessarily also right a wrong, but the practice of making amends does.[1] Amends can be made for damaged property, broken promises, broken trust, parental worry, a damaged reputation, stealing, cheating, or lying.

I like choosing consequences that involve making amends because it teaches children to think about the needs and rights of other people. It helps the child re-bond with the person she has wronged, and it teaches her that mistakes are something to correct. The mother who gave the teenage daughter extra chores to do earlier in this chapter was exercising a creative use of making amends in the consequence. The daughter was forced to experience the consequences of her actions (worrying her mother by coming in late) in a very concrete way: she had to do her mother's chores to make up for the lost sleep.

On grounding: this common consequence usually becomes viable when kids are old enough to play outside with neighbor friends, ride bikes, or go to friends' houses. It may include restriction on phone use or other in-house privileges. Please note, however, that grounding is not a good consequence for a child who likes to stay home with a good book or play basketball alone.

When my son was four, he loved small stuffed animals and would play with them endlessly. We visited some friends one day, and he went upstairs to play with their three-year-old son.

Some fifteen minutes later their daughter, Rachel (11 years) arrived home and began crying loudly, "They ruined them! They ruined them!" I dashed upstairs to find her weeping over five collectible Beanie Babies®—with tags torn off. I went in search of my son, who was hiding under the bed, eyes wide and hands over his ears. Although he knew he was never to take the tags off other people's toys, he confessed that he had found a stool, climbed up to the high shelf where she had reasonably put them, torn the tags off, and played with them. He willingly apologized, but Rachel was still inconsolable.

I told my son that he would need to replace Rachel's Beanie Babies®, and we immediately ordered the replacement toys. He carefully put the toys in a basket and took them to Rachel. He apologized again when he gave them to her. She very graciously accepted them with a hug.

In order for my son to repay me, we made up a chart with lots of dollar signs on it. Every time he did an extra chore for me, he put a sticker on a dollar sign. When he had accumulated enough "dollars," he had worked off his debt.

Jean Illsley Clarke advises only using the amends process for serious misbehaviors since it takes parental time and supervision. You can start the process by asking the child, "How can you fix this?" Younger children will probably need you to make suggestions. Older children can come up with their own ideas. As a parent, you need to approve the plan before it goes into action and supervise its execution. Your child ought to make amends as quickly as possible. If it involves replacing an item that costs money, loan the child the money and set up a re-payment schedule acceptable to you. The victim should not have to wait for the child to earn the money for restitution to be made.

Amends need to be willingly made by the perpetrator and acceptable to the victim. If either of these attitudes are not present, use a different discipline tool to deal with the situation. Along the same lines, if you, the parent, are angry or resentful, it won't work as a teaching tool. Everyone (child, parent, and victim) needs to be satisfied with the restitution.

Parent educators, Linda and Richard Eyre, point out that people grow and mature the most when they correct themselves, learn from their mistakes, and make amends.[2] Therefore it is reasonable to give children many opportunities to correct themselves, ask for forgiveness, and make amends.

One note of caution: do not make amends *for* your child. When a child misbehaves, he ought to feel badly about it and fix it. If you do the feeling bad and making amends, then you deny your child the growth he could achieve in responsibility and conscience.

A WORD ABOUT POWER STRUGGLES

A power struggle is an emotional battle between parent and child over who has control. This is not a pretty place to be, but most of us have found ourselves in such a battle with one of our children at some point. It's important to know that consequences *almost never* work at changing a child's behavior in the midst of a full-blown power struggle. Why? A child who is battling you for power and control cares more about prevailing (gaining or keeping control) than she does about experiencing a consequence. A power struggle can erupt over almost any kind of issue—brushing teeth, picking up toys, cleaning rooms, bicycle boundaries

—you name it. You'll know it's a power struggle and not just a pattern of ordinary misbehavior if:

- Your child does not accept your discipline.
- The battle repeats itself over and over again.
- Both parent and child get very emotional over the issue.
- The parent-child relationship slowly deteriorates.
- The issue is never resolved.[3]

Children get into power struggles because they have a strong inner need to gradually grasp more and more control over their own lives—it's basically the process of autonomy. But sometimes they push for too much, too soon. Parents get into power struggles trying to keep children safe or because they are unwilling to share control. There are many reasons why these struggles happen.

So, if you've got such a power struggle in full swing at your house and consequences are not an option, what are your alternatives? Jan Faull, parent educator and author of *Unplugging Power Struggles*, recommends the following three approaches:

Let go. In areas where the child has ultimate control, like potty training (you can't make someone "go"), back completely out of the struggle. Leave it up to the child.

Offer choices, negotiate and compromise. This is the most commonly-used power struggle resolution technique. Find a way to make it work for both of you. Maybe your daughter wants to ride her bicycle to the store with her friend. You're uncomfortable with that, but will let her go with her older brother, or with yourself several times until you decide she is experienced enough to handle it on her own.

Hold on. In matters of safety or important family values, you do not give in. For example, a child under the age of four must ride in a car seat. Try to give your child a choice within the "no choice" situation. For the child who struggles with the car seat, you can offer her a choice of which toy to play with while she's buckled in.

Throughout Chapter 5 I have noted for you some power struggles you can't win—areas where the child has ultimate control. In general, watch yourself on any discipline issue where your emotions seem to always flood out of control. These are prime areas for power struggles to happen. If you find yourself having a power struggle, use one of the above options to resolve it.

1. Jean Illsley Clarke, *Time-In: When Time-Out Doesn't Work*, (Seattle, WA: Parenting Press, 1999), p. 51.

2. Linda Eyre and Richard Eyre, *Three Steps to a Strong Family*, (New York: Simon & Schuster, 1994), p. 59.

3. See Jan Faull's excellent book on this issue, *Unplugging Power Struggles*, (Seattle, WA: Parenting Press, 2000).

4
DELIVERING THE CONSEQUENCE AND FOLLOWING THROUGH

None of us enjoy our children's misbehavior and all of us feel outrage, disbelief, and indignation at some of it. But when you are first confronted with news of your child's misdeed, or if you are standing right there on the receiving end of it, it pays to stay calm. Parents who frequently lose control of their emotions (losing their tempers, yelling, or crying) abdicate authority and put the child in charge of the situation. The calmer you can be and the more matter-of-factly you act, the more effective your discipline will be.

Envision a parent responding to backtalk by adopting an outraged look and demanding, "What did you say?" This parent is probably in for more of the same. Now envision another parent looking calmly in his child's eye and responding, "That kind of talk is disrespectful. I'm not willing to drive someone to the mall who speaks to me like that," then walking calmly out of the room. In the first example, the parent models a lack of self-control. In the second example, the parent controls his emotions, delivers the consequence, and lets it do the teaching.

I know it's hard. Daily frustration goes hand in hand with parenting. But if you don't control yourself, it isn't fair to expect your child to control his outbursts. When a parent blasts a child with anger, most of the child's energy goes into defending himself against the rage, not into facing the results of his behavior or thinking about what to change next time. And it can scare the child.

> I was running late for a pediatrician's appointment and trying to get both kids' out of the bath, dressed, and out the door. I was also annoyed with my husband for not helping me. My son was complaining and fussing about having his hair dried and my toddler was trying to grab the cord from the hair dryer. I pulled the cord away from her, which caused her to stumble. She started to wail. My son was still fussing. I lost it and yelled for my husband at the top of my lungs. My daughter cried harder and my son looked frightened at my outburst and hid his face in my shirt. My husband showed up and took the baby. I took a deep breath and said to my son, "Come on, let's finish your hair." He lifted a fearful face and said, "Mommy, when you yell like that it makes me feel like you hate me." I resolved then and there to take deep breaths *before* I lost my cool.

For low-energy parents, yelling takes tremendous energy and is very draining. For high-energy parents, it can be a relief to release energy by yelling—however, the child is the one who pays for that relief. Either way, yelling accomplishes little. A raised voice says that you've lost control and are frustrated and powerless.

CALM YOURSELF DOWN FIRST

How do you calm your strong emotional reactions to your children's misbehavior? Here are a few ideas you can use right away. Pick one or two that feel workable to you and practice using them any time you feel your blood pressure on the rise.

Close your eyes and take a deep breath. If you hold your tongue and remember to take a deep breath first, what eventually comes out of your mouth has more of a chance of being governed by your brain than by your feelings. When you experience anger, you can unconsciously hold your breath. No one thinks well without oxygen. Remember to breathe.

Close your eyes and consciously relax your eyebrows, shoulders, and hands. When we tense up, we generally do so in our faces and neck and shoulder area; many people unconsciously clench their fists and teeth. After you've focused on relaxing these areas, open your eyes and begin talking.

Give yourself a time-out. This is particularly helpful when the children are clamoring at you for justice or retribution. Put your hand up in a "Stop" gesture and say, "I need a time-out. I'll speak to you both in five minutes." Then lock yourself in your room or the bathroom and ignore any further fussing. (Consider the age and safety of your children before using this.)

Take a short walk (if the behavior—or results of it—can be safely ignored for a short period of time). Say to your child, "I'm going out to walk around the block. I will speak to you about what you've done when I get back." A quick walk will clear your head and give you a chance to think.

Model controlling your anger. Say quietly, "I am so angry right now that I want to [throw something, ground you for the rest of your life, jump in the river, whatever] but I am going to give myself a little time to calm down. I'll speak to you about this after dinner." This will only work if you can really control yourself and not yell.

Use I-statements. Instead of yelling, "How could you do that?" use an I-statement to let your child know how you feel without blasting him. For example, in a quiet voice, say, "I feel *so* angry and discouraged when I see my child ignoring the no-hitting rule."

Give your child a time-out. Removing the child from the situation (and from your eyesight) gives you a chance to calm down before you speak to her. Say, "Go to your room until I can decide what to do next." Make use of this if you have a tendency to spank.

DELIVERING THE CONSEQUENCE

After you've calmed yourself down and selected a consequence, it's time to deliver the sentence. When you present your child with a logical consequence, don't add any unnecessary words. The shorter you keep it, the greater the impact. Children learn to tune out lectures or warnings about the "next time." Let the consequence teach. Educator and counselor Robert MacKenzie advises parents to practice limiting their involvement to restating the obvious facts: for example, "When you spill your milk, you don't get any more" or "When your curfew is broken, you lose driving privileges" and leave it at that.[1]

COPING WITH CHILDREN'S DIVERSIONARY TACTICS

I guarantee your child will not respond happily to receiving a consequence. She will try any number of tactics to convince you to retreat, withdraw, and back down. Until your children experience a certain amount of consistency and follow-through in receiving consequences and being held accountable to them, they will test whether or not you really mean it.

Here are a few common diversionary tactics and some suggestions on how you can successfully respond (or not) to them.

Tantrums

In response to receiving a consequence, you will see tantrums in the kicking-screaming variety favored by the younger set, the outraged expressions and verbal fits indulged in by older children, and the storming out of the room and door-slamming exhibited by adolescents.

If a child is fussing at you, calmly say, "I'm not willing to talk to someone who behaves like this" and leave the room. Other useful ways to disengage from a tantrum are: "The subject is closed" or "We're done talking about it." Then ignore the tantrum and physically separate yourself from the child. Ignoring communicates to your child your dislike of his behavior. There is no attention payoff from the parent. You leave the child alone to come to grips with the outcome of his behavior. (Be aware that the fussing will probably increase temporarily until the child accepts that it won't get him anywhere.)

Apologies and Second Chances

"I'm sorry, Mommy, I won't do it again!" Promises to do better are a dime a dozen. It's easy to be sorry when you're caught in wrongdoing and facing a consequence. It's not so easy to be handed a consequence and endure the discomfort of it. Don't give in to crying, begging, and pleas for second chances. The misbehavior will likely reoccur and when that happens, you are more likely to *over*react and punish harshly. Children must learn to tolerate the discomfort of a fair consequence. And parents must be willing to tolerate seeing their child unhappy. (If you tend to have a lot of difficulty with this, talk to your partner, a friend, a clergy person, or a therapist.)

Another way to handle pleas for second chances is to tell your child that rules can't be changed *after* someone misbehaves.

Arguments and Protests

"But Dad, that's not fair! I shouldn't be punished when he started it!" Our children seem to come with fully developed arguing skills and little sense of personal responsibility. Parent educator James Jones points out that when a child argues with your decision, he is only interested in explaining his position and pointing out flaws in your reasoning. A child argues in the face of a consequence:

- To delay compliance with your decision.
- To convince you he is right and change your mind.
- To negotiate and bargain out of it.
- To wear you out so you give up and he can "escape."
- To make you suffer and pay before he complies.[2]

You can cut off arguments by saying, "We're done talking about it" or "I've made my decision and I'm not going to change it." If the child persists, say, "If you keep bringing up the subject, I will double the consequence." If he still argues, you must follow through.

Other effective ways to curtail arguments are to essentially repeat yourself as many times as necessary: "Nevertheless, you broke the rule, and you now must pay the price" or "Regardless of how you feel about me..." or "In spite of the fact that you don't think it's fair...." Keep using these phrases and repeating your decision. If you keep calm, your child will run out of steam.

When a child argues that a consequence is unfair or too harsh, say, "Anyone who thinks it's okay to do [whatever misbehavior child indulged in], is in *no position* to judge what is right or wrong in a consequence."

Some parents worry that their child may not really understand the rule, or that there may actually be extenuating circumstances and the argument may be legitimate. I would point out that if your child is really interested in discussing your rules, the best time to do it is not when those rules are being broken. Set up a later date (two or three days later) to talk about the household rules— perhaps at a family meeting. Put a note on the refrigerator or calendar to be sure the family gets back to it (if you fail to do this, you give your child the message that her needs and concerns are not so valuable as yours). If the argument is solely for diversionary purposes, it won't be quite so impassioned by the time you actually sit down to a family meeting. If the argument *is* valid (be open to this possibility), then give due time and attention to renegotiating the rule.

The motive behind diversionary tactics is to get you to withdraw the consequence and abdicate parenting. Regardless of your child's efforts to get you not to, it is your job to parent. Stand firm and calm in the face of these storms. Use the calming techniques described earlier in this chapter. Remind yourself that you do your child no favor by giving in.

THE IMPORTANCE OF FOLLOW-THROUGH

Follow-through means that once you have given the consequence, you must enforce it. If that means staying

home one afternoon to make sure a grounded child doesn't
sneak out, then so be it. If you tell a child she may not
have after-school snacks for three days and then look the
other way when the neighbor offers her a cookie, you will
lose credibility in your child's eyes.

Making exceptions to a rule, for example, failing to give
a consequence when a child has broken a house rule or
failing to enforce a consequence given, disrespects the rule.
If the rule has too many exceptions, children eventually
discover that it is not really a rule after all. If you establish
rules and then do not enforce them, your children will learn
that you cannot be depended on.

You can expect your children to test your limits and
rules. It is the only way they can find out if you really
mean what you say. Children put greater stock in what you
do than in what you say; telling them isn't enough—they
need to be shown that you will follow through. Parent
educator John Rosemond puts it this way,

> When a child breaks a rule, a parent must impose
> discipline. This gets the child's attention and says, "See, we
> were telling you the truth."   Consistency is therefore a
> demonstration of parental reliability. Consistency frees child-
> ren from the burden of having to repeatedly test rules. In-
> consistency causes children to keep "gambling" because they
> can't predict when they'll "win."[3]

Physical Follow-Through

With young children you will often need to physically
help them comply with your consequences. For example,
I often tell my young daughter that she can walk to the car
or I can carry her. Usually she chooses to hold my hand
and walk, but occasionally I have to carry her to help her
comply.   Physically following through sometimes means
restraining a child in the throes of a tantrum so that he

doesn't hurt himself or anyone else. It should be gentle, yet firm.

THE NEXT STEP

In the next chapter you will have a chance to do some planning for specific behavior problems your children are exhibiting now.

1. Robert MacKenzie, Ed.D., *Setting Limits: How to Raise Responsible, Independent Children by Providing CLEAR Boundaries,* rev. ed., (Rocklin, CA: Prima Publishing, 1998).

2. James Jones, *Let's Fix the Kids!* (Westminister, CA: Familyhood, 1997).

3. John Rosemond, *John Rosemond's Six-Point Plan for Raising Happy, Healthy Children,* (Kansas City, MO: Andrews & McNeel, 1989), p. 52.

5
COMMON MISBEHAVIORS AND EFFECTIVE CONSEQUENCES

This chapter lists some of the common misdeeds children commit, the natural consequences for the deed (if any), and approximately two to seven possible logical consequences for that behavior. The following is a brief table of contents:

The misbehaviors are organized alphabetically and ranked by what I call their Level of Offensiveness:

Level 1 = Annoying or obnoxious, but not too serious

Level 2 = Important to address, but not earth-shattering

Level 3 = Unsafe, immoral, or simply intolerable.

What is a level two for me may be a level three for you if you find that behavior intolerable, so feel free to alter my rating system using your own values. Rating the seriousness of the misbehavior can help you choose a consequence that is proportional to the offense instead of to your emotion at the moment or your level of built-up irritation.

I have included tips on preventing the misbehavior, notes of caution, or references to other parenting techniques that work well. Remember, not every problem needs to be solved with a consequence.

Lastly, you will note that a few of the consequences listed are not logically related to the misbehavior. They are included because enough parents listed them as effective consequences, despite their unrelated nature. My suspicion is that the occasional unrelated consequence works because it matters greatly to the child (for example, many parents rated loss of Nintendo™ privileges as very effective, no matter what the crime). I don't dispute that an unrelated consequence can work, but I do assert that related ones work better at effecting long-term change in the child's behavior. Read on.

WON'T FOLLOW THROUGH ON ACTIVITY/LESSON
COMMITMENTS (won't practice, protests going to lessons)

Level of Offensiveness: 2 = Important to Address

Natural Consequences: None

Logical Consequence Possibilities:
■ Say, "We made a promise to the teacher to pay for six months of lessons. If you won't practice, then you need to help pay for the lessons with your allowance."
■ Set a consequence ahead of time. If child misses a set amount of practice, you take him off the team.
■ Child must write a letter of apology to coach/instructor for missed practice.
■ Say, "If you don't want to go to practice, fine. I won't make you and I won't be mad at you if you want to quit the team. But understand this, if you decide not to go to practice, it means you're quitting the team. We won't be going back at all. Make sure that's really what you want to do." Then leave the room and let her think about it. (Only use this option if you really are willing for her to quit the activity.)

Other Thoughts:
■ Make sure the lessons or activity is something the child really *wants* to do. Sometimes we handpick our child's activities and facilitate them without really finding out if the child enjoys them. Sometimes a child is talented at something but doesn't particularly like it, or is simply tired of doing it.
■ Be sensitive to the fact that the only way a child can find out if she likes an activity is to try it. Part of childhood is trying out different sports and activities to see what one

enjoys or is good at. If she really doesn't like a certain activity, then quitting may be appropriate.

■ A child may need extra help from you during the initial learning process to feel confident enough to continue. Many parents routinely practice batting, shooting baskets, or kicking a soccer ball around with their youngster.

■ Be open to negotiation, especially with older children. If you've required your son to take piano lessons for five years, be willing to listen when he wants to stop. If piano is important to you, offer a compromise. One mom told her eleven-year-old son if he continued piano lessons till the end of the school year, she would let him take the summer off. At the end of the summer, they would decide together if he would begin lessons again.

SQUANDERS ALLOWANCE (buys junk and skips lunch at school)

Level of Offensiveness: 2 = Important to address

Natural Consequences:
■ Doesn't have money for legitimate needs or wants (lunch, movies, etc.)

Logical Consequence Possibilities:
■ If child was accustomed to buying lunch at school, she now makes her own at home and carries it to school.
■ Loss of entertainment (no funds to go to skating rink or movies).
■ Loss of having allowance. If your child is having trouble handling the responsibility of an allowance, she probably isn't ready for one.

Other Thoughts:
■ Don't give more allowance than you are willing for your child to squander, especially while she is learning to manage it herself.
■ Do not rescue child. She must cope with the natural consequences and forego the privilege of buying lunch. Many children have trouble learning to budget their money, especially at first, so help her learn.
■ You have the right to veto any purchase that is unhealthy, unsafe, or violates your values.

ARGUES A LOT WITH PARENT

Level of Offensiveness: 2 = Important to Address

Natural Consequences: None

Logical Consequence Possibilities:
- Say, "Parenting is my job. If I let you [whatever she wishes to do or avoid] then I wouldn't be doing my job. I have to do my job, regardless of how you, or anyone else feels about it." Then ignore any further arguing. Leave the room, if necessary.
- Disengage and ignore. Say, "Nice try. My decision stands. I'm not going to argue." Then ignore.
- If child argues for more than 30 seconds, she must go to her room for a set amount of time. Make this a standing rule for repeat offenders.
- Loss of privileges (friends, TV, video/computer games) for the day, after one warning.

Other Thoughts:
- Arguments are usually sparked by a parental "No" in response to something the child wants to do, or they are an attempt by the child to avoid something she must do. Occasionally, your older child will have a legitimate argument with one of your rules or decisions. Be sensitive to these times, but insist that the discussion be respectful and occur when both parties are calm (i.e., not in the midst of a rule violation).
- If your child frequently makes the protest, "It's not fair! Why do I have to...(or) So-and-so doesn't have to....", educator Thomas Lickona, author of *Raising Good Children,* recommends responding with something like the following. "It's a matter of [love, responsibility, obligation], not

fairness. Sometimes we do things strictly out of fairness, but other times we do things because it's the right thing to do, or it's the loving thing to do, or it's the respectful thing to do. This is a time when I need you to think of others instead of yourself."[*]

■ If arguments are a standard part of your family's day, consider having weekly family meetings where the household rules and family plans are discussed and negotiated ahead of time. (See page 21 for more information on how to use family meetings.)

See also: Discussion of arguments and protests on page 52

---

[*]Thomas Lickona, Ph.D., *Raising Good Children: Helping Your Child Through the Stages of Moral Development*, (New York: Bantam Books, 1983).

MISBEHAVES FOR BABYSITTER

Level of Offensiveness: 1 = Obnoxious

Natural Consequences:
- Sitter who won't come back.

Logical Consequence Possibilities:
- Next time sitter is scheduled to come, put child in bed before sitter arrives (plan to leave a bit before child's regular bedtime). Child must stay in bed the whole time sitter is there.
- Charge your child for "combat pay." For an older child to whom money matters, say, "Since you misbehaved for this sitter last time, we have to pay her more to watch you. You will pay the extra money."* (If you are in the habit of using a teen sibling for a sitter and the younger ones misbehave, hire an outside sitter and collect the sitter's fee from the misbehaving children.)
- Bedtime next day is earlier.
- (For child who enjoys sitters) Next time child is required to go on boring errand with parent instead of staying home with siblings and sitter.
- Must apologize to sitter.
- Not allowed to participate in next day's activity with family.
- Confine child to the house for one day.

---

*When you charge your child money as a consequence, don't deduct it from the child's allowance or take gift money. That's not money he has had to make any effort to get. Instead, take money he has earned or require him to do extra jobs to pay for the misdeed.

Other Thoughts:
- Make sure your children know ahead of time what behavior you expect while the sitter is there. Review the rules each time you go out and remind them of the consequences if they misbehave.
- It's possible you have a bad match between the kids and the sitter. Consider finding one who copes better with your childrens' temperaments.

BACKTALK

Level of Offensiveness: 3 = Intolerable

Natural Consequences: None

Logical Consequence Possibilities:
- Instant removal from family activity. Say, "That kind of talk is not acceptable. It tells me you don't want to be here with us." Send to room and ignore any fussing.
- Say, "Those kinds of words [or that kind of behavior] is disrespectful and abuses my time, energy, and goodwill. Because of this I am no longer willing to [drive you to soccer practice, serve you dessert, allow Nintendo™ for the evening, buy you those new shoes, or whatever privilege your child was counting on enjoying next]." Use a very calm, matter-of-fact tone when you do this and then immediately leave the room or separate yourself from your child and his inevitable reaction.
- Child must apologize to parent.
- Give one warning, then loss of privilege most cherished by child (video games, friends over, etc.) for the day.
- Loss of outing privileges for the day.
- Loss of playdates for 1-3 days.
- Send to room.

Other Thoughts:
- Children try backtalking because they are looking for ways to feel important and will often find it in power-seeking and attention-getting behavior. I've rated this offense as intolerable because, unchecked, backtalk can become a serious problem where children lose the necessary respect they must have for their parents and gain an inappropriate amount of control in the home. Although

individual instances of sassiness or impertinence can be minor, a steady and escalating pattern of backtalk needs to be taken seriously and dealt with firmly. The best consequence for this behavior is as related to the offense as you can make it, and delivered immediately. For an excellent discussion of this discipline problem, see Audrey Ricker and Carolyn Crowder's book, *Backtalk*.*

■ I've found it useful with my children to interrupt the backtalk and say in a warning tone, "Wait. Start over." If they check themselves and speak respectfully the second time, I let the incident pass.

■ Ask calmly, "Do you really think that tone of voice will get you what you want?" If the child rephrases the comment respectfully, let it pass. If he does not, proceed with a consequence from above.

■ A two-year-old (or younger) child who shouts "No!" at you is not backtalking. Saying "No" is necessary to a young child's development. It's best to simply ignore the "No", pick her up and proceed with whatever you need to do.

■ I used a "Voice Improvement" chart with my five-year-old son. He received a star every time he made a request or comment respectfully. If he used an unpleasant voice or backtalked, he received a black check mark. He then had to earn an extra star to cover up the black check. When all boxes were filled with stars, he got to go out to lunch with his favorite cousin. The chart didn't get rid of all the problems, but it helped him pay attention to how he used his voice, and it reminded me to notice when he spoke respectfully.

---

*Audrey Ricker, Ph.D., and Carolyn Crowder, Ph.D., *Backtalk: Four Steps to Ending Rude Behavior in Your Kids*, (New York: Simon & Schuster, 1998).

USES BAD LANGUAGE (bathroom words, cursing)

Level of Offensiveness: 2 = Important to Address

Natural Consequences: None

Logical Consequence Possibilities:
- For bathroom talk, say, "Since you need to use bathroom words, I will take you into the bathroom to say them." Stand in the bathroom with her and tell her she can use all the potty words she wants. This will soon take the fun out of bathroom talk.
- If your child swears at you, calmly say, "I don't appreciate hearing the word [#*?!]. Because you have not treated me respectfully, I don't feel motivated to...take you to dance class, make cupcakes with you, go shopping for tennis shoes" (whatever the child is looking forward to doing next). Repeating the swear word calmly takes much of the drama out of its use.
- Removal from family (or social) activity. Say, "Those are words we do not use in our family. Go to your room until you're ready to use better language."
- If the child is hearing the bad language on TV, then forbid those particular programs. Pay attention to the cartoons your child is watching—many are extremely inappropriate.

Other Thoughts:
- Bathroom talk is pretty prevalent around four years of age—usually just used among the child's friends. The phase passes most quickly when you ignore it.
- Sometimes, giving a child an acceptable alternative to cursing when she's frustrated can be helpful. For example,

you might allow expostulations of "Oh, crabgrass" or "Sassafras!" or nonsense words.

▪ Children often use swear words when they hear them regularly. If they're hearing them at home, the grownups need to dramatically clean up their act. If they're hearing them at school, explain to your child that swear words demonstrate a lack of maturity and self-control; it's "show-off" behavior.

WON'T GO TO BED (or, gets up repeatedly)

Level of Offensiveness: 2 = Important to address

Natural Consequences:
- Child gets overtired.

Logical Consequence Possibilities:
- Set the timer. If child isn't in bed by the time it rings, he loses a "bedtime privilege" (bedtime story, backrub, reading or listening to story tape in bed).
- Say (to older child), "Since you're not tired enough for bed, you can do the dishes."
- If she gets out of bed, put a baby gate on the door to keep her confined to the bedroom. (If your child is a climber, you might put two gates on top of each other.) Make sure the room is safe. You can put blankets and pillows by the gate if you think she will fall asleep there. Ignore any crying. The rule is: Get up and the gate goes up for the night.
- If child gets out of bed, the door closes (or the night light gets turned off). If he stays in bed, the door stays open.
- One hour earlier bedtime the next night. Or, however many minutes the child is late to bed, then double that for the earlier bedtime the next night.
- No bedtime story that night (or the next) if she gets up.
- Each time parent has to escort child back to bed, one toy gets removed from the room. Toy stays out-of-reach for one day.
- Loss of TV time the next morning.
- If child makes a habit of appearing at parents' bedside in the night (scary dream, lonely, whatever), she can sleep with a blanket on the floor beside the bed. If she gets into their bed, she is escorted back to her room.

Other Thoughts:
■ Independent sleeping skills (the ability to put yourself to sleep and back to sleep) are important life skills. The problem may not be disobedience, but rather, lack of learning. Your young child may not know *how* to put himself to sleep. There are many things you can do to help your child learn these skills, such as bedtime rituals, attachment to loveys, and setting limits.*
■ After the bedtime ritual, it is useful to promise to come back in 5-10 minutes and "check" on the child. Make good on your promise, even if she is asleep.
■ Some parents take away a pacifier if the child won't stay in bed. I don't recommend it since *many* children use pacifiers as "loveys" or as an aid in getting to sleep. Leave the pacifier be.
■ Use a reward. If the child is in bed early, he gets an extra 15 minutes reading time before lights-out.
■ Use a routine and chart. Once child has checked off all the pre-bedtime tasks (put on pajamas, brush teeth, etc.), she can read or be read to until her predetermined lights-out time. If she gets done quickly, there's lots of reading time, if not, there's little or no time to read. This works well because the "bad guy" is the clock—not Mom or Dad.
■ Lastly, be aware that you can do all the above things perfectly, but you can't control whether or not your child actually goes to sleep. Your child holds ultimate control here, so don't get into a power struggle over it—you'll lose. Find a technique effective at keeping your child in her bed, with lights off (night lights are okay). Tell her, "You must

---

*See *The Sleep Book for Tired Parents* by Rebecca Huntley, (Seattle, WA: Parenting Press, Inc.,1991) for useful ways to address major sleep problems.

stay in your bed, but you are in charge of when you close your eyes and sleep." Then leave her to it.

BEGS AT THE STORE

Level of Offensiveness: 1 = Annoying

Natural Consequences: None

Logical Consequence Possibilities:
- Each child gets to select one agreed-upon item (cereal, gum, ice cream flavor); if she begs for another item, she gets to choose which one she wants to keep; if she begs a third time, she loses all items.
- Make a rule: If you beg for it, the answer is automatically "No."
- Anyone who begs at the store must go home; just leave the grocery cart and take the child home. Do this when the other parent is available to sit with the child or resolve to do your shopping at another time. You will probably only have to do this once to convince your child you are serious.
- Say, "My ears don't hear begging" and then ignore it.
- A chronic beggar loses the privilege of going to the store with you.

Other Thoughts:
- Give an occasional, intermittent reward for not begging. Say, "I really appreciated how you both didn't ask for things in the grocery store. I'm stopping at the pet store on the way home and we can visit those puppies you like."
- Make your expectations clear. Before you go into the store say, "We're only going to buy the things on my list. You may not ask for any treats. You may help me pick out the [whatever item you need]."
- Never, ever buy your child candy at check out. It just teaches her to beg for it every time. (I've been known to

say, "Only grandparents buy candy at the check out."
Their grandparents love to do this and I don't mind.)

▪ My sister tells her small children that they're allowed to
smell the candy at the check out, but not allowed to touch
any. She reminds her two year old not to touch by saying,
"Put your hands behind your back."

▪ If a child begs and won't take your first "No" for an answer, make eye contact and say clearly, "I've made my
decision and I'm not going to change it."

▪ Have your child sit down with you and help write out the
grocery list. Let her decide which healthy snacks you will
buy. Then have her find them in the grocery store. All the
"asking" needs to happen at home making the list. Any
asking at the store gets a "No."

▪ Reflect the child's feelings. Say, "You *really, really* want
that Super Sugar Bomb cereal, and you're disappointed that
we're not buying it."

BLAMES OTHERS (excessive focus on "who started it")

Level of Offensiveness: 2 = Important to Address

Natural Consequences:
- Damage to friendships and sibling relationships.

Logical Consequence Possibilities:
- Put the child in a time-out corner, or some other boring, quiet, not-too-cozy place. Tell him that he can't come out until he can tell you what *his* contribution to the problem was. You will likely need to help your child see his part in the conflict the first few times you do this.
- Refuse to listen to "who started it" tales or to solve the problem for the children. Say, "It takes two to fight. I'm not interested in who started it. I'm only interested in who can solve it." Tell them they can sit in separate corners until they each have two ideas on how to solve the problem. (The younger child should be three or older in order to use this technique. Expect to help guide them in this process until they get the hang of it. See note below for help in teaching children problem solving skills.)

Other Thoughts:
- Don't just administer discipline. Teach your child about conflict resolution and problem-solving. Give him the skills he needs to resolve problems himself.[*]
- Children who are, by temperament, easily frustrated often feel incapable on many levels. Therefore, they tend to

---

[*]See Elizabeth Crary's *Kids Can Cooperate* and the *Children's Problem Solving Series* in the bibliography for practical help with teaching children how to solve their own conflicts.

blame others whom they see as more competent. Continually look for ways to help this child build competence; for example, help them break a big task down into small parts.*

See also: Tattles, Mistreats sibling

---

*For more information on this temperament style, see Helen Neville and Diane Clark Johnson's *Temperament Tools* (Seattle, WA: Parenting Press, 1998).

MISBEHAVES IN THE CAR (argues over seats, won't keep seatbelt on, fights with sibling—"He's looking out my window!" "She's breathing my air!")

Level of Offensiveness: 1 = Annoying (fighting)
                            3 = Unsafe (takes off seatbelt)

Natural Consequences:
- Possible injury if not wearing seatbelt.
- Unsafe driving conditions.

Logical Consequence Possibilities:
- Any fighting results in loss of "kid music" on the tape player.
- Anyone who breaks the car rules (i.e., No fighting) has to clean the car upon arrival home.
- Show them you will follow through. Schedule a trip somewhere fun: out to eat, to the toy store, to look at puppies at the pet store, etc. Once fighting breaks out, cancel the outing. Turn around and immediately go home.
- A fighting child loses her window seat.
- If anyone's seatbelt is not buckled, the car stops.
- If child takes off seatbelt, tie seatbelt in place with an additional cord child can't unfasten. Say, "When you take off your seatbelt, the tie goes on."
- If older child does not have seatbelt buckled before car starts, charge him a fine (enough to hurt a bit).
- Loss of next privilege child expects when you get home.
- Require both children to be silent and sit with their hands folded in their lap.
- Send to room (or bed) when you get home.
- Pull over in a safe place. Put the squabblers outside the car. Stand there with them, but don't pay any attention to them.

- Stop the car and refuse to drive until everyone is quiet.
- Separate the children, if possible.

Other Thoughts:

- When good behavior is evident, reward the children: praise, small treat, stop for ice cream, etc.
- Review your car rules frequently. For example, Seatbelts buckled, No quarreling, No throwing, Keep your hands and feet to yourself, You can only ask "Are we there yet?" once. Remember to notice *good* car behavior and comment on it.
- Avoid children fighting for a certain seat in the car by either establishing assigned seats, a rotating seat system (certain child gets it on certain days of the week), or the person with the most "yucky" chore that week gets the coveted seat. The front seats are really much less safe for children, even if you *don't* have airbags installed in your car—it's better to not have your children in the front at all. Make it a standing rule.

PROTESTS CHORES OR REQUESTS (argues, whines, bargains)

Level of Offensiveness: 1 = Annoying

Natural Consequences: None

Logical Consequence Possibilities:
- Protests earn the child another chore. Keep adding chores until the protests stop.
- Give a choice of chores. If he still protests, tell him, "I guess you'll be doing both then."
- Instead of talking, physically take the child by the hand and lead him to the chore. Then leave him to do it.
- Say, "The longer you put the job off, the longer it will be until you get to [play with friends, ride bike, whatever child wants to do]."
- Any arguing means the immediate loss of discretionary activities (sports, dance, outside play, etc.) for the day.

Other Thoughts:
- Turn a deaf ear to the protests; do not respond at all. When the child starts to do the chore, immediately thank him for cooperating.
- Do not allow child to leave the site of the chore until it is done.
- At another time, discuss the family chore assignments. If he finds one chore particularly distasteful, he may be able to exchange it for another task. Do not, however negotiate this trade on the spot after whining and protesting.

See also: Argues a lot with parent, Discussion of arguments and protests on page 52

DOES CHORES POORLY

Level of Offensiveness: 2 = Important to Address

Natural Consequences:
- Inconveniences or annoys family members.

Logical Consequence Possibilities:
- Child must leave whatever she is doing and "re-do it right."
- Pick child up from school, bring her home and have her re-do the job until satisfactory. If there are consequences for missing class, the child must assume responsibility for them. (Use this for a chronic problem and after one warning.)
- Reduce allowance.
- Child must re-do chore and also do one of yours.

Other Thoughts:
- Make sure your child has the necessary skills to do the job. Teach the chore properly in the first place and then provide support as she practices. Until your child is competent at a chore, don't just send her to do it. Go with her and work alongside until you are confident she can do the job adequately. Reduce your standards while your child is learning a new skill. Find at least one thing to compliment about the job and praise progress or improvement made. Do not criticize while your child is learning.
- Many parents put more emphasis on the quality of work than the fact that the child made a contribution to the family. If all the child hears is criticism, it's not going to result in much improvement. Progress, no matter how small, is to be praised. Do not punish progress because it isn't "enough" or doesn't meet the goal right away.

- If your child truly hates a certain chore, consider switching her to another job. For example, my husband loathed doing yardwork as a child. It set his hay fever off and he was miserable all day long. He says he would have been more cooperative about doing an inside chore.

FAILS TO DO CHORES

Level of Offensiveness: 2 = Important to Address

Natural Consequences:
- Rooms are messy and difficult to use.
- No clean dishes.
- Overflowing garbage—no place to put new garbage.
- No clean clothes.

(Unfortunately, all of these natural consequences matter far more to parents than they do to children. Most parents rely on logical consequences or rewards to make a difference here.)

Logical Consequence Possibilities:
- Establish house rules:
    1. No privileges may be enjoyed until chores are complete.
    2. Undone chores = loss of privileges for the next day.

Those privileges could be:

TV/Video game time	Playing with friends
Computer time	Allowance (reduce it)
Sports activities	Planned outings

- If child fails to set table, everyone sits at the table and waits until she sets it.
- Wake child who fails to take out the trash at 10 or 11pm and have her do it then.
- Say, "Hmmm. If you are reluctant to do your chores, you must need more practice doing them to feel comfortable. Here's another chore to give you extra practice."
- "I forgot" is often an evasive way of saying, "I didn't want to." Tell your child, "I notice you didn't forget to watch your favorite TV show or to call Jamie on the phone. I don't believe you forgot. I believe you just didn't do it." Then restrict one privilege for 1-3 days.

- If a child fails to do a chore and you have to do it, charge her a fee (charge enough to make it hurt a bit). Say, "If you expect other people to do your chores, then you should expect to pay for it."
- Take child to the site of the undone chore and tell her she must stay right there until it is done.
- Clothes that don't get put in hampers don't get washed.
- If the children fail to set table, clear table, do dishes, etc., then the kitchen is not ready for the next meal. Parents (only) go out for the next dinner.
- Anyone who won't participate in family clean up must sit alone on a couch (or other very boring spot) until chores are done by others.
- No food (snacks) until chores are adequately done.

Other Thoughts:
- Establish a chore routine. When you do this, chores become more like a habit. People put off tasks more easily than habits.
- If you have regular chores, establish deadlines for all of them. Post them on a chart so no one can conveniently "forget" the deadline. Establish consequences in advance for failing to meet the deadline.
- Sometimes legitimate forgetting happens when there are many steps to a task. For example, there are many parts to cleaning up a bedroom—putting away clothes, making the bed, sorting and putting away toys, organizing papers and books, closing closet doors and dresser drawers, etc. Make a list of the tasks and have the child check off each one as she completes it.
- Don't continue to accept "I forgot" as an excuse. Notice that the child doesn't forget to do things she likes to do. Say, "I'm sorry you forgot, however you will still need to

complete the chore. To help you remember next time...
[give consequence]."
▪ Being able to work and make a contribution to the well-
being of the family is a crucial step to healthy self-esteem.
Chores are really the only concrete way a child can make
such a contribution. Don't just throw in the towel on this
one; it's important to your child's growth. If you're having
a lot of trouble getting your child to do one particular
chore, consider switching him to one he finds less distasteful.
The idea is to have him contribute to the family, not to
gain expert skill in, say, trash hauling.
▪ Parent educators report that troubles with chores are
typically ongoing in families. Don't be surprised—or too
depressed—to have this problem crop up regularly as you
raise your children. Be prepared to use different strategies
and consequences as your children grow and change.
▪ I highly recommend taking a look at the chart on page
51 of *Pick Up Your Socks* by Elizabeth Crary. This chart
shows the average ages children do specific chores with
help, with reminding, and independently. It helps to adjust
your expectations of the child's performance and responsibility for the chore.*

---

*Elizabeth Crary, *Pick Up Your Socks...And Other Skills Growing
Children Need*, (Seattle, WA: Parenting Press, Inc., 1990).

MISBEHAVES IN CHURCH

Level of Offensiveness: 2 = Important to address

Natural Consequences:
- Other church-goers are bothered.

Logical Consequence Possibilities:
(For young children)
- Take out for a talking-to and then go right back in (give no opportunity to run around or play).
- If child is too loud or rambunctious, he loses his "church toy" or snack.
- Remove from chapel and hold child firmly on your lap until behavior changes. Then go back in.
- (For the child who wants to stay with you) If a nursery is available for your age child, tell him that if he misbehaves, he goes to the nursery. (If you're working on *getting* the child to stay in the nursery, then don't use this as a consequence.)

(For school-aged children)
- Plan a special outing for after church. Those children who behave are allowed to go. Others go home.
- Write a letter of apology to pastor or speaker.
- Later that day child is confined to her room for however long she misbehaved in church.
- For each reminder to behave, child receives an extra chore at home.

Other Thoughts:
- Expecting very young children to behave well in church (sitting still, being quiet) just isn't realistic. Adult church services are not very interesting or understandable for little people. Many three year olds have trouble sitting still for

even five minutes. A large percentage of school-aged children find it hard to sit still for an hour. This doesn't mean you shouldn't take them to services, but it does mean you need to be prepared. Bring coloring books, small, quiet toys, books, and snacks to keep small children occupied during a sermon. Plan to take them out a couple times. For younger children, sit in the back where the wiggling around won't disturb others. For older children, sit in the very front and center where they won't be distracted by their friends.

▪ Make your expectations clear. Review your "church behavior" rules before you go in (for example, Keep your body calm, Use a whisper-voice).

▪ Use hand signals to quietly communicate with your children. A finger to the lips means, "Be quiet." A palm flat out says, "Stop." Pointing to your eyes and ears can mean, "Look and listen." You can also make up signs for "Stand" and "Sit." Teach these signals at home and then use them during the church service.

▪ If your school-aged child can tell you one thing he learned from the sermon, he gets a treat afterwards.

▪ My husband and I cope by noticing other children's misbehavior in church; it helps us to realize we're not alone.

CARELESS WITH PERSONAL ITEMS (loses coat, shoes, lunchbox, etc.)

Level of Offensiveness: 2 = Important to Address

Natural Consequences:
- Child then does without that item.

Logical Consequence Possibilities:
- If item is retrievable, child must pay adult's gas mileage for taking him back to the place it was left to find it. (Child could use money to repay adult or do a job.)
- If this is a recurring problem, sell something of the child's in order to pay for a replacement. For example, have him pick out two video games to sell in order to pay for a new coat. (A variation on this is to withhold allowances to pay for a replaced item.)
- For mild climates: if child loses a coat, he must then buy an inexpensive sweatshirt and show that he is responsible with it before the coat can be replaced. For colder climates: have the child buy a much less expensive coat (*not* stylish) —maybe from a thrift store—and do the same as above.
- Child must purchase replacement with his own money.
- If child repeatedly fails to lock up his bike, you lock it up for him—with a different lock—no bike riding for a week.
- Consider withholding an outing that calls for a coat.

Other Thoughts:
- Whenever possible, don't rescue the child by replacing the item. The natural consequence of not having a favorite item is a tremendous teacher. You can express sympathy for the loss, but don't lecture or say, "I told you so."
- If you live in a cold climate, it isn't safe to let your child go without a coat to experience the natural consequences.

Some parents will then get a light jacket for the child so he can experience the natural consequence (be uncomfortable, but not dangerously cold).

■ Try rewarding your child for the times he *does* remember to bring his coat, shoes, bike, etc. home. Plan two small rewards for the next week.

IS CRITICAL OF OTHERS (put-downs, gossips)

Level of Offensiveness: 2 = Important to Address

Natural Consequences:
- Erodes relationships.
- Damages reputations.

Logical Consequence Possibilities:
- Set a rule in your family. Only helpful talk is allowed. If you hear one of your children criticizing a sibling, ask, "Will that comment help your sister or discourage her?" After one such warning, require the critical child to make amends (she could do a chore for her, assist her with whatever task she was criticizing her proficiency at, etc.)
- If you hear unkind gossip in your home, tell the child to stop and then review the natural consequences of gossip (see below). If you hear a second offense, require the child to apologize to the person being gossiped about.
- If put-downs or criticisms are common in your household, require the offender (child or parent) to put a donation into a "family event" bank. Save up for something fun the family can do together.

Other Thoughts:
- Have a discussion with your child about the natural consequences of put-downs. They reveal a speaker's insecurity; she puts people down because she doesn't feel good about herself. Even if the target laughs off the put-down, inside she doesn't like it, won't forget it, and will likely get

even the first chance she gets. Put-downs cause others to think less of you and avoid you.*

■ Talk with your children about the harmfulness of gossip. It can damage someone's reputation, completely color how a person listening to gossip views a person he hasn't met, spread false information, and cause a lot of pain. Tell them, in your house, you discuss someone not present as if that person were standing right next to you, listening. If you can't say something in front of her, then it shouldn't be said behind her back.

■ Most children care about their parents' good opinions; a statement like, "I'm very disappointed to hear you talk like that. I expect better from my children" will have an impact. Let your parental disappointment function as a natural consequence.

■ Do not model gossiping or put-downs. Do not participate passively in gossip by listening to it. Let your children hear you stop gossip directed toward you by holding up your hand in a "Stop" gesture and saying, "Wait. I don't think I should hear this" and then change the subject. Teach them to do the same or walk away if others do not stop harmful gossiping.

---

*Thomas Lickona, Ph.D., *Raising Good Children: Helping Your Child Through the Stages of Moral Development*, (New York: Bantam Books, 1983).

CUTS CLASSES

Level of Offensiveness: 3 = Intolerable

Natural Consequences:
- Poor or failing grades.
- School consequences.

Logical Consequence Possibilities:
- For a first (minor) offense, loss of privileges (TV, phone, outings, friends, babysitting) for one week.
- Say, "Since I can't trust you to attend your classes, I will be accompanying you to classes for [1-3] days." Get permission from the child's school and do it. Use this option after one warning.
- Get daily attendance records from the school each week. (Or make up an attendance chart and have your child get each teacher to sign it each day she attends class.) On Friday, look at the chart. If your child's attendance record is perfect, she retains all weekend privileges. If she has unexcused absences (or "forgets" to bring the chart home), then she loses all weekend privileges and is basically grounded to her room.
- Child must make up missed work after school with a teacher or at home with you. No other discretionary activities allowed until work is completed.
- Child must apologize to the teacher of the skipped class.

Other Thoughts:
- Point out to your child that cutting class is essentially lying and sneaking around. It is a violation of trust her parents and teachers have in her.
- Ask your child why she's cutting classes. Is it a mild case of spring fever or is she not interested in the relevance

geometry will have in her life? Ask her what she *wants* to learn about. Try to arrange for her to take some kind of class or instruction in an area of personal interest.

DAMAGES PROPERTY (accidentally, or on purpose)

Level of Offensiveness: 2 = Important to Address

Natural Consequences:
- Damage to items.

Logical Consequence Possibilities:
- If child is able, he must repair the item.
- If child cannot repair item himself, then he must pay to have it fixed or replaced. If he has no money, he must do extra chores to earn it.
- Make amends by doing jobs for the parent.
- If parent repairs the item, child must do jobs for the parent to free him up for doing the repairs.
- If child is unwilling to make amends, consider selling a toy to pay for the broken item.

Other Thoughts:
- If your child has a pattern of breaking things on purpose, look for the underlying problem. Is he having trouble expressing his anger appropriately? Is there some other stress that is getting vented here? Talk to the child and do a little investigating. Instead of using your energy being mad, help him to make amends and then work with him on managing his anger in a constructive way.
- The consequence of paying for or replacing something becomes more meaningful when the child must put forth effort to do so. Therefore, using money the child has worked to earn teaches more than just using allowance or gift money.

See also: Throws things when angry

DAWDLES

Level of Offensiveness: 2 = Important to Address

Natural Consequences:
- Could get left behind.
- Not finishing schoolwork can result in poor grades.
- Morning-dawdler goes without lunch because there wasn't time to make it.

Logical Consequence Possibilities:
- Loss of outing child is not ready for. Say, "We'll go another day."
- If child isn't dressed when it's time to go, he leaves the house in his pajamas (he can get dressed in the car). Use an advance warning; either set the timer or say, "Be dressed by the time the bell rings, or you get in the car in your pajamas." If he still doesn't comply, say, "I see you chose to go in your pajamas" and pick him up and go.
- If your school-aged child dawdles and misses the bus (or just won't make it on time), tell him it's too late to go to school. Give him an unending succession of chores to do until school is out (rake leaves, scrub floors, weed, etc.)
- If your child makes you late by not being ready, then he must make amends by doing one of your jobs later that day.
- Set timer. If child isn't ready when bell rings, he loses a privilege or gets an extra chore for that day.
- If child is a morning dawdler (and likes eating), require him to have all his morning tasks done before he is allowed to eat breakfast.
- If child dawdles at the table, take away his plate at the "exit" time. No snacks until the next meal.
- Dawdling in the morning results in loss of afternoon privileges (like TV or computer time).

Other Thoughts:

■ Make use of your kitchen timer. Set it for a certain time and tell your child he needs to be ready when it goes off.

■ Use a star chart of tasks and times they must be done by. Give small, daily rewards.

■ If the child doesn't like to be late to a class or activity, remind him, "Five minutes till we leave. Are you ready?"

■ Turn off your TV. It's distracting to everyone.

■ Make mornings easier. The night before, have child set out clothes for the morning, make school lunches, braid long hair before bed, put on next day's underwear (or even clothes!), and put books and papers in backpack.

DEFIES PARENT ("No!" or "You can't make me")

Level of Offensiveness: 3 = Intolerable

Natural Consequences:
■ Angry parent.

Logical Consequence Possibilities:
■ Say, "You can do it now, or spend 15 minutes in your room getting ready to do it."
■ Say, "You must need extra practice at this task since you're so reluctant to do it" and give an additional related chore, or double the first request.
■ For a child who says, "You can't make me!" matter-of-factly answer, "You're right. I can't make you [do your homework, brush your teeth, etc.] but I can make your life mighty uncomfortable until you decide to cooperate. It's your choice." If the child remains uncooperative, remove the next privilege the child is planning on enjoying.
■ For a young child, physically assist her in complying.
■ Loss of item or activity child was involved with and send to room until an apology to parent is made.
■ Time-out (for those children truly out-of-control).
■ For an older child, take away the very next privilege or activity she was counting on doing. For example, calmly say, "I do not appreciate your lack of cooperation, and now I don't feel motivated to cooperate with getting you to the skating rink." (You really have to follow through here, or this just becomes an empty threat.)

Other Thoughts:
■ How consistently you follow through on your rules will make a difference in how much defiance you will have to deal with. A child who finds that defiance works at getting

rid of a parent's requests even *some* of the time will try it again and again. A child who has tested the waters a few times and found no payoff is less likely to use it.

■ If your child is prone to defiance, it may be a combination of temperament traits that are colliding to cause the trouble. For example, a persistent, slow-adapting, intense child will feel driven to defiance more often than an easy-going, flexible personality type. If you suspect this is the case for your child, you will find help in many of the good parenting books that are available on temperament and guidance.*

■ Young children usually need more time to mentally process a request or direction from you. It may not be that she is ignoring or defying you, but rather taking in what you said. Silently count to five before you expect your child to respond.

■ Some children use defiance in order to engage you in a fight. Stay calm, deliver the consequence dispassionately, and then leave the room. Arguing, yelling, or the like will only give her what she's after—a conflict with you. Remember, debating your rules during the midst of a rule violation is a bad idea. Talk with her later when you're both calm.

■ A pattern of defiance can be an indicator of a power struggle going on. If a power struggle is underway, do not use consequences. (See page 44 for further information on power struggles.)

■ Give an immediate second chance to comply. Look your child straight in the eye and say, "Let's try that again.

---

*See *Understanding Temperament* by Lyndall Shick, (Seattle, WA: Parenting Press, Inc., 1998) and *Temperament Tools* by Helen Neville and Diane Clark Johnson, (Seattle, WA: Parenting Press, Inc., 1998).

Kate, put your shoes on." Many children will see you mean business and cooperate.

See also: Backtalk

HAS FRIENDS OVER WITHOUT PERMISSION

Level of Offensiveness: 3 = Possibly unsafe

Natural Consequences:
- Loss of parental trust.

Logical Consequence Possibilities:
- For older, latch-key child, say, "Since I can't trust you when you're here alone, I guess you will have to be watched and supervised." If you work, hire a babysitter or enroll your child in an after-school program. If you're an at-home parent, require your child to accompany you on all errands for a period of time.
- Send the friends home immediately.
- Loss of playdates, privilege of seeing friends (perhaps even phone contact) for one week.

Other Thoughts:
- This tends to be a problem for older children. You can prevent it by letting your children (and their friends) know your rule and consequence ahead of time. You can also regularly ask your child's friends if their parents are aware of their whereabouts; if not, send them home immediately to ask for permission to be there.
- Explain to your older child that you are legally responsible for all that happens in your house. If he entertains friends and someone is hurt, *you* are liable. If he insists that he makes safe decisions, you can say, "Oh, I trust you. But you can't control another person's behavior."
- For a child who likes to protest, "You don't trust me!" Educator Thomas Lickona advises responding, "Trust isn't

blind; it's based on knowledge. I need to know where you are, who you're with, and what you're doing."*

■ Instead of banning everyone from crossing your threshold, consider selecting one calm, responsible friend who is allowed in the house for a limited time during your absence.

---

*Thomas Lickona, Ph.D., *Raising Good Children: Helping Your Child Through the Stages of Moral Development*, (New York: Bantam Books, 1983).

HOMEWORK HASSLES (doesn't do it, forgets it at school, procrastinates, doesn't finish it, does it carelessly, tries to get parents to do it)

Level of Offensiveness: 2 = Important to Address

Natural Consequences:
- Can result in poor grades.
- School consequences, such as detention, or loss of recess.

Logical Consequence Possibilities:
- All privileges (TV, phone, video games, sports practice) dependent upon completed, satisfactory homework (must be checked by parent).
- If done carelessly, must re-do homework (from the beginning) until satisfactory.
- If she tries to get parent to do homework, she forfeits parent's legitimate assistance for the rest of the week.
- If she procrastinates a lot, she loses next privilege she was anticipating, such as soccer practice (even if she manages to get done in time).
- If any homework from the preceding week is left undone, no weekend privileges until it's finished.

Other Thoughts:
- Set a house rule: No discretionary activities until homework is done. Adhering to and following through on this rule will help prevent many homework problems.
- For the child who wants too much help from you, limit your involvement by saying, "I'll watch you do the first problem" or "Read the directions for the problem to me."
- Sometimes children get into a homework-avoidance loop when the work really is too hard for their skill level. Consult with the teacher and get extra help.

TELLS LIES (or, won't own up to wrongdoing)

Level of Offensiveness: 3 = Intolerable

Natural Consequences:
■ Loss of parental trust.

Logical Consequence Possibilities:
■ For the rest of the day, refuse to believe anything the child says. When he gets upset, say, "Well, you told me a lie today. Now I can't believe anything you say. Unless you *always* tell me the truth, I don't know when to believe you."
■ For a serious lie, restrict any privilege requiring parental trust (playing unsupervised, going out with friends, riding bikes out of your eyesight, etc.) until the trust is re-earned.
■ Give one consequence for breaking a rule, then add another (or double the consequence) for lying about it.
■ Loss of all discretionary activities (phone, TV, outings, friends) until child owns up, apologizes, and makes amends.
■ Grounded to room until he accepts responsibility and owns up, or for the rest of the day.

Other Thoughts:
■ Children typically lie for one of four reasons: to avoid punishment, to avoid an adult's anger (or nagging), to cover up for inadequacies or embarrassment, or because they are so young they don't yet know the difference between truth and fantasy. All children discover at some point that a convincing lie circumvents punishment. What they don't know, however, is what kind of long-term damage lying does to their characters and to relationships. A serious, eye-level talk about how lying destroys trust and hurts the

relationship between parent and child will help prevent further dabbling in lying.

■ Don't invite lying by asking, "Did you...?" when it's pretty obvious he did, or by asking, "Who did it?" If two or more children are together they will often blame the littlest or the one with the worst reputation. Instead, say something like, "Honey got spilled on this couch. We need to clean it up."

■ Keep in mind that lying is more common in homes where spanking is used.

■ If you suspect your child is lying out of fear of your anger, try saying something like, "If you've done something wrong and you're afraid to tell me because you think I'll be mad, I want you to say, 'I'm worried you might be mad about this...' and that will remind me to stay calm. You might have to make amends for the problem in some way, but I'll be very proud of you for telling the truth." Then when your child comes to you in this way, make sure you do stay calm.

WON'T EAT MEALS ("I'm not hungry" or, insults the cook—"This tastes yucky!" "Carrots again?")

Level of Offensiveness: 1 = Annoying

Natural Consequences:
▪ Child goes hungry.
▪ Cook doesn't feel like cooking anymore.

Logical Consequence Possibilities:
▪ If you complain about your food, you lose the privilege of eating that meal. Say (with a smile), "Okay, you don't have to eat. I'm sure you can make it to the next meal," and send child to his room. No snacking before next meal.
▪ Make amends to the cook. Explain how disheartening it is to prepare a meal and then have a family member insult it. Ask the child to think of a good way to make it up to the cook.
▪ Say, "If you're not hungry enough to eat your [disliked item] then you're not hungry enough for dessert."

Other Thoughts:
▪ Many parents don't mind a child choosing not to eat a disliked dish, but require him to not say *nothing* about it and simply leave it on his plate. This way a younger sibling does not receive coaching on which foods to dislike.
▪ Set some limits. Say, "This is dinner. After we're through eating this, the kitchen is *closed*." The child can eat at the next meal (nothing till then). Or, serve the child teensy-tiny portions of everything (or have him take as many tiny bites as his age). He may not complain or make faces. He doesn't have to eat everything, but he may not have seconds of anything until he finishes his original plate of food. If he complains, use a consequence from above.

■ Teach (or review) table manners with your child. Give him two or three ideas on what to say when he is served or offered something he doesn't care for. For example, he could say nothing and simply leave it on his plate, or he could say, "No thank you. May I have extra potatoes instead?"

■ Lots of parents recommend having your child plan and prepare dinner once a week. When they make it themselves, they like eating it a lot more and hopefully, become more sensitive about making comments on others' menu selection and cooking. Children as young as four can learn to cook. You will need to assist them as they learn, but by age ten, most children are able to prepare and serve simple meals. Note: when helping children with meal preparation, honor their menu choices (within reason—no ice cream for dinner) and make sure everyone eats what they make.

■ Lastly, be aware that you can't *make* a child eat. Since this is an area where the child has ultimate control, it is also a common area for power struggles to occur. If mealtimes are becoming emotional battles at your house, limit your use of consequences to behavior at the table; don't give consequences for not eating. Power struggles around food and how much a child eats can encourage eating disorders.

MISSES DEADLINE FOR RETURNING HOME

Level of Offensiveness: 2 = Important to Address

Natural Consequences:
- Loss of parental trust.

Logical Consequence Possibilities:
- For each 15 minutes late, the next day's deadline is shortened by 15 minutes.
- Child cannot leave the house/yard the next day.
- (For teen) Loss of driving privileges for 3-7 days.
- (For teen) Set an alarm clock in parents' room for the late-night curfew. When teen comes home, he must turn clock off. If he misses curfew, alarm goes off and wakes up parents. He must then report in and explain himself to his tired, worried, crabby parents.

Other Thoughts:
- Explain to your child that we owe our greatest courtesy to the people we live with. It is not courteous to be late and worry those who love us.

NONVERBAL DISRESPECT (door slamming, dirty looks, ignoring parents)

Level of Offensiveness: 2 = Important to Address

Natural Consequences: None

Logical Consequence Possibilities:
- For a minor offense, completely ignore child. Give the behavior no attention at all.
- (If child frequently slams bedroom door) Take the door off the hinges and put it in storage for 1-3 days. Say, "Since you are abusing the privilege of having a door, it will be taking a well-deserved rest. You can dress in the bathroom. If you refrain from slamming other doors during this time, you can have your door back." Note: do not take the door away permanently.
- Send to room. Child can't come out until a reasonably sincere apology is made to parent.
- Require child to write you a letter of apology, explaining why this behavior is insulting and inappropriate.
- Send to bed for an enforced nap of one hour.

Other Thoughts:
- This kind of disrespect is just a nonverbal form of backtalk.
- Acknowledge the emotion of the gesture. Say calmly, "I see you are feeling [irritated, disappointed, upset, etc.] Do you really think that gesture [or look] will get you what you want?"

See also: Backtalk, Defies parent

REPEATEDLY ASKS THE SAME QUESTION (or, states the same information over and over again)

Level of Offensiveness: 1 = Annoying

Natural Consequences: None

Logical Consequence Possibilities:
▪ Respond with a question, "What did I tell you the last time you asked that?" Child must repeat the answer. Or ask, "What do *you* think?" Then instruct the child not to ask again or he will lose a privilege.
▪ If child asks more than two times, he loses a privilege.

Other Thoughts:
▪ Young children do this because they don't like the answer they've gotten (for example, "No, we can't go to the park today"); they're bored or overexcited ("Are we there yet?"* "Is it time to go?"); or because they're focusing in on a fear or issue common to their developmental level ("Are there sharks in our swimming pool?")
▪ Older children do this not so much by asking the same question over and over again in one day, but by asking questions to which they already have the answers to. This isn't so much an attempt to be annoying as it is a clumsy way to initiate a conversation on a topic the child is interested in, or just an attempt to engage a parent's attention. If the child is interested in a topic, read a book on it together, watch a documentary, or do an internet search *together.* If it's just attention the child wants, teach

---

*See also, Misbehaves in the car

him how to ask for it in a more appropriate way—and then spend the time together (or commit to a time when you will).

MISBEHAVES IN RESTAURANTS

Level of Offensiveness: 2 = Important to Address

Natural Consequences:
- Other diners are bothered.

Logical Consequence Possibilities:
- Give one warning and then leave the restaurant. This is very effective for the child who likes to eat out—especially if he doesn't get to finish his meal. You'll likely only have to do this once.
- Loss of next dining-out event.
- Time-out in lobby or car (accompanied by parent who gives them no attention) or in an empty booth next to you.

Other Thoughts:
- Make your expectations clear. Talk about your restaurant rules before you go in and what will happen if they are violated.
- Small children need to *learn* how to behave in restaurants. Plan to dine at family-oriented restaurants and expect several difficult trips while they learn the rules.
- Avoid the problem of hunger while waiting for food by giving your child a light snack before you leave, or order something that will arrive quickly, like a glass of milk.
- Bring small toys or paper and crayons for quiet entertainment.

WON'T CLEAN ROOM

Level of Offensiveness: 1 = Annoying

Natural Consequences:
- Can't find things.
- Can trip over items on floor.
- Clothes don't get washed.

Logical Consequence Possibilities:
- Have a standing rule: Take care of your things or you lose the privilege of having them. If a child fails to clean his room by the agreed-upon time, select a few favorite items off the floor and put them in storage for a week (1-2 days for younger children).
- Messy rooms are dangerous for people to be in, therefore no friends are allowed over to play or spend the night until it is cleaned.
- If room is not tidy by bedtime, then no story.

For chronic offenders:
- If you are good at getting rid of clutter (ie., tossing things), tell your child *you* will clean the room for him. This usually motivates a packrat or a disorganized "collector" of treasures to get started.
- Post a warning sign on the door: "Room off-limits until cleaned." Child has one day to address the problem. At the deadline, parent inspects the room. If it passes, child can use the room again. If not, the room remains off-limits except for cleaning. Every time the parent inspects, he charges an inspection fee. (If the child disrespects this process, buy a locking door knob and keep the door locked except for cleaning.) This is a big consequence. I would recommend bringing up the subject and plan at a family

meeting before implementing it. (See page 21 for a discussion of family meetings.)

■ Pack up everything on the floor (or out of place) in small boxes. At the end of each week the child may have one box back, provided he has kept his room tidy each day that week. A variation on this is to put all the items in storage (hidden from child) for 1-2 weeks.

■ The older child who persistently refuses to keep his room clean loses the privilege of having a bedroom. It can become Mom's exercise room or Dad's study for 1-3 days. It is off-limits to the child. If he enters the room, then the off-limits time is extended another day for each offense. Again, this sort of consequence needs airing in a family meeting first. If you plan to use it, ample warning needs to be given.

Other Thoughts:

■ Cleaning a whole, messy room feels overwhelming to most children. Help them break the job down into smaller pieces they can handle. Post a checklist of tasks so they can check them off as they do them. Stay with them, supervise, and be supportive as they work.

■ Establish a daily (or weekly) clean-up time. No discretionary activities are allowed until the clean-up is done.

■ Remember to notice and praise a child for a neat room, or even certain neat areas of a room.

■ Many children do not appreciate orderliness and cleanliness until they live with it for a while.

■ Don't accept the common statement, "It's *my* room and I should be allowed to keep it any way I want." The child's room is in your house, legally belongs to you, and should conform to your (reasonable) standards.

■ One way to help a clutterbug/packrat keep order in her room is to get her a large, oversized scrapbook. After she cleans her room every Saturday, have her put all important or sentimental papers and keepsakes in the scrapbook. All else gets pitched. She will learn to pick and choose what's really meaningful to her.

▪ It's always easier to keep a room in order when there is less "stuff." Some families regularly clean out children's rooms and decide together which items to donate to charity.

▪ Children today collect an *immense* amount of toys. One mom took everything out of her six-year-old daughter's room. She gave back anything her daughter could remember and asked for. Everything else was kept in boxes in the garage. After a few months, the mom donated anything left unasked-for to charity.

▪ Don't get into a wholesale power struggle with your child over the state of her room. If the problem has expanded to this level (emotional arguments every day), then consequences are not the way to solve it. See page 44 for a brief discussion on resolving power struggles.

See also: Won't pick up toys

REFUSES TO GO TO ROOM (or, won't stay in room)

Level of Offensiveness: 1 = Annoying, obnoxious

Natural Consequences: None

Logical Consequence Possibilities:
- Say, "You can go now or I can take you and double the time you spend there." Make compliance the easiest choice for the child. Note: this will work with ages three-to-four and up. A two year old cannot yet understand this concept.
- Say, "If you stay in your room, the door stays open. If you come out before (the timer goes off, you are calm, etc.) I will put you back in and close the door."
- If child leaves room, the time spent there starts over.
- If child tries to leave room, parent holds the door closed for the required time.
- Restrict child's favorite privilege and then escort child to his room.

Other Thoughts:
- Make use of your kitchen timer when sending a child to his room. That way he just needs to listen for the bell, and you are out of the loop.
- Some adults remember that being sent to their room wasn't so bad, but it inspired more repentance when Mom or Dad came in to talk with them when the time had been served. Make this talk calm and focused not on what went wrong, but on *how to do better* next time. Reassure the child he is loved.

See also: Defies parent, Backtalk

RUNS OFF ON OUTINGS

Level of Offensiveness: 3 = Unsafe

Natural Consequences:
- Child could get lost or injured.

Logical Consequence Possibilities:
- Child must ride in stroller. (If you're in a store, put the child in a shopping cart.)
- Child must wear harness (a good option for a child who is very physical or needs to spend the energy).
- Plan a test outing. Go to the park or someplace she really likes. When your child runs off, retrieve her and put her back in the car. Say, "When you run away from me, we go home."

Other Thoughts:
- Review your rules for outings frequently with your young child. Before you get out of the car, say something like, "Now remember, you need to hold my hand (or the stroller, or Mom's pocket, or older sibling's hand) while we walk through the parking lot. When we get inside Daddy's office, you can walk by yourself as long as I can see you."
- When you're juggling bags, children, and car keys, it's difficult to get the car open and still keep track of your kids. Some parents find it useful to tell their young children to put their hands on the car while they unlock it. Another option is to give the child the unlocking job; that way, he's occupied in a safe spot.
- If this is a recurring problem, make sure you've taught your child what to do if she gets lost. I frequently remind my children of the following: If you get lost—

Stay where you are till Mom comes to find you.
If Mom doesn't come, find a clerk/uniformed person and
  ask for help.
If you can't find a clerk, ask a woman with small
  children to help you.*

It's also helpful to point out the "Lost Children" station to
your children at theme parks, carnivals, and other large,
busy places. Older children can often be trusted to meet
you there if you get separated.

---

*See the Elizabeth Crary's Children's Problem Solving book
I'm Lost (Seattle, WA: Parenting Press, 1996) for additional ideas
on getting lost and found.

SAYS, "HUH?" OR "WHAT?" A LOT

Level of Offensiveness: 1 = Annoying

Natural Consequences: None

Logical Consequence Possibilities:
▪ Ignore. Respond to "Huh?" or "What?" with silence. If your child rephrases her response respectfully (for example, "I'm sorry, Mom. What did you say?"), then repeat your request.
▪ Require your child to make the extra effort. Respond to your child by saying, "Tell me what I just said to you." You will be surprised how often the child has really heard the gist of what you said.
▪ If this is prevalent when the TV is on, then turn off the TV for five minutes each time your child answers, "Huh?"

Other Thoughts:
▪ This is a habit that frequently crops up at about age eight. It is mostly just that, habit and a bit of laziness. Many children train their parents to repeat themselves three or more times before they bother to pay any real attention. Don't let it get to that point.
▪ If your child is one to get very engrossed in something, then make sure you have her attention before you make your request. Say, "Chelsea, please look at me." Make eye contact and then talk. Or, you can touch your child gently to get her attention before you speak.
▪ Watch your own habits of inattention and response here. How many times do your children have to repeat themselves before you pay attention to them? I have this problem myself, especially if I'm reading something or involved in a project that takes thought. Teach your

children how to politely interrupt you and then reward them with your immediate attention when they do so.

■ I explained to my stepson, who is very bright, that saying "Huh?" all the time made him sound unintelligent. Then I told him that I would not be responding to a "Huh?" in order to remind him to answer people more politely. He still forgets himself from time to time, but corrects himself promptly.

MISBEHAVES AT SCHOOL

Level of Offensiveness: 2 = Important to Address

Natural Consequences:
- School consequences, such as loss of recess, detention.

Logical Consequence Possibilities:
- Must apologize to teacher and acknowledge what she did wrong (verbally or by letter).
- Arrange with teacher to receive a weekly report on your child's daily classroom behavior. For each behavior offense he loses one weekend privilege.
- Loss of one privilege (for 1-3 days) for each offense.
- Playtime restricted for 1-2 days.

Other Thoughts:
- Remind your child of what appropriate classroom behavior is: No talking with your neighbor, Listen to the teacher, Stay in your seat, etc.
- Conference with the teacher. Find out which behaviors are recurring and work with your child on curbing those.
- A star chart to reward good behavior would help here. Use daily behavior reports from the teacher.
- A highly-active child may have extreme difficulty staying in his seat. This is more temperament than misbehavior. Withholding recess would only make matters worse in this case. Work with the teacher at helping find ways for your child to spend energy in ways that do not disrupt the class.

See also: Blames others

NEGLECTS SELF-CARE (school-aged child: bathing, getting dressed, tooth brushing)

Level of Offensiveness: 2 = Important to Address

Natural Consequences:
- Unwashed, smelly child.
- Tooth decay.

Logical Consequence Possibilities:
- Say, "Because I had to spend my time doing for you what you are able to do for yourself, you will have to do these chores of mine this afternoon." (Choose something the child will not enjoy doing.)
- If child does not brush her teeth, she is not allowed to have any sweets until she demonstrates 5-7 days of responsible brushing.
- If your child fails to wash her hands before dinner, take her plate off the table till her hands are washed.
- No breakfast until child is dressed and ready to go in the morning.
- Child is allowed to do nothing else until self-care task is finished.

Other Thoughts:
- For a child who wants help with something she can do for herself, say, "You get started and I'll be there shortly." Let the child do the majority of the task by herself. If this works, it's probably attention from you she's after. Meet this need in other, more appropriate ways. If it's simply a disinclination to stop playing and do what's necessary, then use a logical consequence.
- For those children who are looking forward to a visit from the tooth fairy, tell them that she is *most* generous to

those children who have properly cared for their teeth. When the tooth fairy first visited my son, she left a note for him saying she really wanted nice, sparkly clean teeth to build a castle with, so could he please remember to floss more?

▪ Ask your dentist for disclosing tablets which show where children aren't brushing well. Have your child chew one periodically—after brushing—so she can see where she needs to improve.

▪ For young children who are easily frustrated, getting dressed by themselves can be a long, hard task. Lay the clothes out for her in the direction she will put them on (shirt face down, pants face up). Have her dress near you so you can lend a hand, if need be.

▪ Check your standards. A five year old may be able to dress to her own standards, but not to your's. Except maybe for church and special occasions, accept your child's standards. It's better that the child feel successful on a daily basis. Her standards will gradually improve.

▪ Power struggle alert #1. Many families get into power struggles over teeth brushing (probably because parents wish to spare their children the natural, painful consequence of tooth decay). If you are having daily battles getting your school-aged child to brush, you might choose to just do it for her for the time being and give everyone a chance to calm down. Try again later, maybe use a reward chart to motivate her instead of consequences.

Very young children are a different story. Dentists say children under the age of eight really need an adult to brush for them, or at least finish the job. Buy child-sized tooth brushes (or get them from your dentist) and fun kid-flavored toothpaste. There are even little creature-shaped flossing sticks on the market to use on children. Make it fun.

■ Power struggle alert #2: I haven't included toileting in this section because consequences are generally not appropriate to use in this area. However, it is a very common issue for parents and children to get into big power struggles over. Remember, you can't *make* a child go to the bathroom; she has ultimate control here. If you're having daily battles in this area, drop back and read one of the many good books on toilet training. I recommend *Mommy! I Have to Go Potty!* for an excellent discussion of potty training power struggles.*

---

*Jan Faull, *Mommy! I Have to Go Potty!* (Hemet, CA: Raefield-Roberts, Pub., 1996).

WON'T SHARE TOYS

Level of Offensiveness: 1 = Annoying

Natural Consequences:
▪ Damage to friendships and sibling relationships.

Logical Consequence Possibilities:
▪ Parent removes toy and sets timer. If the children don't come up with a solution on how to share or play with it together by the time it rings, the toy is unavailable for the rest of the day.
▪ Enforced sharing: set timer for five minutes. Children take turns with toy.
▪ If someone has grabbed the toy away without asking, that child must make amends.
▪ Toy is put away for one day (reduce time for young children). Nobody gets it during this time.

Other Thoughts:
▪ Not all toys must be shared. Let children have a few special toys that are allowed to be theirs exclusively. A lovey or a brand-new toy are items that should not have to be shared.
▪ Substitute another toy for the one being fought over.
▪ With young children, it is useful to have at least two of any popular item. Then each child can have the same toy.
▪ Say, "Looks like we have a problem. How can you solve it?" Solicit the children's input. For some good problem

solving ideas, see the Children's Problem Solving story *I Want It* for lots of good ideas on teaching children to share.[*]

■ Have your child put away any special toys she's unwilling to share before her friend comes over.

■ Get down on the floor and model how to take turns and share toys with your child. Parents are easier to share with because they are more willing to compromise and are sensitive to the child's cues. Along these same lines, buy yourself a few fun toys and keep them in your room. Model sharing by allowing your child and her visitors to borrow them.

---

[*]Elizabeth Crary, *I Want It*, (Seattle, WA: Parenting Press, Inc. 1996).

MISTREATS SIBLING (physical aggression—hitting, kicking, tripping, spitting, biting or verbal aggression—name-calling, unkind teasing, or outright tormenting)

Level of Offensiveness: 2 = Important to Address

Natural Consequences:
- Damages sibling relationships.

Logical Consequence Possibilities:
- Since it takes two to tango, say, "I see you two need practice in getting along." Get out a board game and require them to play 1-3 rounds (or 10-20 minutes) while you monitor the play—require kind, respectful interaction.
- Require child to make a list of at least three things she can do instead of hitting when her sibling bothers her. List must be made before child can do any discretionary activity.
- Say, "Bothering your brother is not making good use of your time. Here's something constructive you can do" (give an unpleasant chore like taking out trash. If the child complains, give an additional chore).
- Say, "Since you're not treating people kindly, you will not be able to have your friend over tomorrow."
- Make amends. Child must do sibling a kindness or tell her two reasons why she loves her. Say, "You really hurt your sister when you [called her names, shoved her down, whatever]. Now what can you do to help her feel better?" (See page 42 for a discussion on how to help children make amends.)
- Not allowed to play with sibling for next 5-10 minutes.
- Not allowed to play alone with sibling for one day or until sibling agrees to play again.
- (For spitting) Say, "Because you want to spit, stay in your room until you fill up this medicine cup with spit."

- Both children must go to a time-out spot and stay there until they can tell the parent what they themselves did wrong (not what the other child did), apologize to the sibling, give him a hug or handshake, and promise to try to do better.
- Child must do one of her sibling's chores.
- Both children get sent to their rooms for 30 minutes. It doesn't matter who started it. The third time they get sent to their rooms, they stay there the rest of the day (except for bathroom trips and meals).
- (For namecalling) Child must re-phrase her comment 2-3 times in a respectful way.
- (For namecalling) Charge a fee. Child who was insulted gets the money.
- Loss of participation in next activity.
- Physically restrain the offending arms or legs for a few minutes.
- Time-out (separate the children).
- If child feels any remorse for the teasing, have her apologize to sibling.
- Send to room for specified time (use timer)—up to one hour for older child.
- Loss of TV/video game privileges—one day for each offense.

Other Thoughts:
- A certain amount of parental teaching is in order before consequences will truly teach young children in this situation. Preschoolers need to learn how to connect a sibling's facial expressions and words with feelings. Parents need to explain how to recognize when a sibling is hurt or upset and help the child understand why she shouldn't cause such hurt.

Similarly, children ages 6-11 need to have their attention drawn to the feelings of others. This age range can be very insensitive to others because they can't *see* the hurt name-calling causes inside another child.

▪ Be careful of forcing a child to apologize. Be reasonably certain the child is really sorry before having her apologize or it can just encourage her to lie. Some children also figure out that if they quickly say they're sorry they can get away with something; it's not a matter of remorse, just evasion of responsibility. Instead of requiring an apology, focus on making amends.

▪ A standing family rule against mistreatment and name calling will help prevent this problem. Children eventually begin to treat others in the same way they treat their siblings. You must teach respectful behavior toward others in your home and enforce it.

▪ When dealing with the aggressor, it can be helpful to ask questions to get him to think and learn. For example, "Ryan, what's the rule in our house about hitting? Why do we have that rule? What would happen if we all ignored that rule?"

▪ For a young child who has a problem with hitting, teach her to stop herself as her hand goes up and to scratch her head instead. Reward her when she remembers to do this.

▪ Remember, children of different ages are working on different developmental skills—such as establishing boundaries and using personal power. The most convenient person to practice these skills on is a sibling. It can be helpful to you as a parent to figure out what the teaser is really after—is he feeling powerless in other relationships and taking it out on this one? Is he bored and looking for a little excitement?   How effective your response is will depend on what the child's goal is.*

■ Be aware that the bigger/older sibling often will take unfair advantage of the younger/smaller one. The younger sibling commonly manipulates or provokes the bigger one into trouble. Although an individual incident may clearly point to one child being at fault, the larger picture usually reveals both parties' participation.

■ Some children have a tendency to interfere in a sibling's discipline (acting hugely victimized, glorying in the aggressor's downfall, or just excessive hovering).   If this happens, give the interfering child the same consequence.

■ Some children who have just been hurt in some way will turn around and sabotage the sibling's discipline by defending him or trying to protect him.   Again, you can give him the same consequence as the aggressor, however, be aware this child needs your help learning certain skills: how to notice when a sibling is getting mad, when to leave the room, how to ask for help from grownups, etc.

---

*See Elizabeth Crary's helpful book on this topic *Help! The Kids Are At It Again: Using Kids' Quarrels to Teach People Skills*, (Seattle, WA: Parenting Press, Inc., 1997).

POOR SPORTSMANSHIP (losing and fussing/crying, winning and bragging, refusing to play if there's little chance of winning)

Level of Offensiveness: 2 = Important to Address

Natural Consequences:
■ Damage to friendships: other children begin to dislike or avoid playing with child.

Logical Consequence Possibilities:
■ Loss of participation in next game.
■ Give one warning if poor behavior occurs during play. Second time, immediately remove child from game.
■ Child must apologize to coach, team, or person he has insulted.
■ If poor behavior results from watching his favorite teams lose, then restrict TV. If it happens while playing board games with others, then restrict board games.

Other Thoughts:
■ A four or five year old can get very upset when losing at a family board game. This is because instead of feeling like he has lost a *game*, he feels like he is a lesser *person*. Avoid this by offering the choice of playing by the game rules or the child's "own" rules. In the latter case, he will probably always win, but that's okay because it's up front and in the open (he's not cheating).
■ Make sure you're providing enough non-competitive activities that emphasize collaboration, yet offer the same sense of accomplishment that winning does—for example, tossing a ball back and forth with a parent, shooting hoops together, creating buildings out of blocks, or doing a puzzle together.

■ Establish rules for winning and losing: Winners can't tease losers or crow too much over their victory; Losers can be sad, but can't yell and slam doors, etc.   Explain that a good winner is one who behaves modestly and that a good loser is someone who accepts the outcome calmly, doesn't blame others for what happened, and is gracious to the opponent.

■ Teach your child the rules of being a good sport:
1. Take the game seriously—no clowning around.
2. No refereeing (don't point out rule violations or criticize others' play).
3. Play your own position (don't try for other kids' shots).
4. Praise others' good plays or efforts ("Great shot" or "Nice try").
5. If you win, pretend winning isn't that important to you.
6. Finish the game—even if you are losing or tired of playing.*

■ Avoid asking, "Did you win?" or "Did you score?" Praise effort and good sportsmanship. Ask questions like, "Did you do your best?" or make comments that note improvement, like, "I can really see how you've been practicing kicking—that kick you made in the second half was great."

■ If a line call is marginal, teach your child to call it in favor of the opponent. Explain that this is honorable and protects his integrity (he will develop a reputation for being fair and players will trust him).

---

*The rules of being a good sport are drawn from Dr. Fred Frankel's excellent book, *Good Friends Are Hard to Find,* (Pasadena, CA: Perspective Publishing, 1996).

■ Give child practice at home in playing games with you. Starting around age four, children can start to cope with losing occasionally. Work with him at learning to lose gracefully. Reward him whenever he displays good sportsmanship.

■ Watch some TV sports with your child and point out instances of good and poor sportsmanship.

■ Post this poem by sportswriter Grantland Rice somewhere conspicuous in your home.

> When the One Great Scorer comes
> to write against your name,
> He marks—not that you won or lost—
> but how you played the game.

STEALS (takes things from stores without paying)

Level of Offensiveness: 3 = Immoral, illegal

Natural Consequences:
▪ If caught, can be prosecuted for shoplifting.

Logical Consequence Possibilities:
▪ The classic, time-tested consequence is to take the child back to the store, have him return the item and apologize to the manager. If child has eaten the item, he is required to pay for it from his own money.
▪ Restrict child from being in *any* store: young child—1-2 weeks, older child—30 days.
▪ In addition to being required to return item and apologize, restrict child from whatever item he stole for a period of time—for example, no candy for one week.

Other Thoughts:
▪ Most children will try stealing a small item from the store (candy, usually) between the ages of four and seven. Parent educators generally advise you to treat such an episode seriously, but know that it probably doesn't mean your child is embarking on a life of crime. If you take care that your child learns a lesson at this early age, the memory of the experience will stay with him and discourage him from trying it again later. The deed is more serious when older children steal or if any age child repeatedly steals.
▪ If a store clerk or manager does not properly address the stealing (says, "That's okay" or a mere "Just don't do it again") then you need to do more. Have a serious talk with your child about why stealing is wrong. Have him write a letter of apology to the store, in addition to the verbal apology. Apply another of the consequences listed above.

■ Explain to your child that stealing is a violation of trust and respect between him and the store owner. Would he like it if the store owner entered his bedroom and stole one of his belongings? What would happen if everyone stole from the store? Try to stretch your child's moral thinking here to stimulate a higher understanding of the immorality of stealing.

WON'T SIT STILL AT THE TABLE (wiggles, gets up and down)

Level of Offensiveness: 1 = Annoying

Natural Consequences: None

Logical Consequence Possibilities:
▪ If child leaves the table without being excused first, she's not allowed back. Make sure a young child understands this rule (use a warning) before enforcing it.
▪ Child must sit at the kitchen counter (or small table nearby) by herself to finish her meal.

Other Thoughts:
▪ Table manners includes more than just how we eat our food. Teach your children to sit on their backsides, squarely on the chair, knees pointing forward. Teach them how to courteously ask to be excused to use the bathroom or when finished.
▪ Studies have shown that homes with regular family dinners produce stronger families and well-adjusted children. Make meals a time of family togetherness and communication rather than allowing toys or reading and writing material at the table (this goes for adults too!)

TAKES THINGS WITHOUT PERMISSION

Level of Offensiveness: 2 = Important to Address

Natural Consequences:
- Angry owner of "borrowed" item.

Logical Consequence Possibilities:
- Child is not allowed to legitimately borrow anything for 2-3 days.
- Make amends to the owner of the item. Say, "Your brother is really upset you took his sweatshirt without permission. What can you do to help him feel better?" (Child might offer to loan him something special of his own.)
- Child must pay a rental fee for the item taken.
- For a young child, take away the item (cookie, off-limits toy, whatever). Say, "No cookies for the rest of the day."
- If a young child has taken something from a friend's house, she must immediately return the item and apologize. If it happens again, restrict playdates for 1-2 days.
- If item is damaged, child must repair or replace it using her own money.

Other Thoughts:
- This would be a good time to have a discussion about the value of respect. If we want others to respect our things, we must also respect the belongings of others. Remind children of the golden rule: Do unto others as you would have them do unto you.

TANTRUMS (screaming, kicking, throwing a verbal or physical fit)

Level of Offensiveness: 1 = Annoying, obnoxious

Natural Consequences:
- Child could get hurt.
- Friends might not want to play.

Logical Consequence Possibilities:
- Loss of whatever item or object caused the tantrum.
- Parent locks self in own room until child is calm for several minutes. (Do this only if you are sure your child won't hurt herself, anyone else, or any property.)
- If the tantrum occurs in public, child must stay with a boring babysitter for the next outing.
- Send to room until done fussing—hold door shut, if necessary. Child must be calm for several minutes before she may come out. If she trashes her room while there, she must clean it up before she can come out. Any abused items disappear for a couple days.
- If in public, leave and go home immediately. Child loses a privilege when you get home.
- Time-out to a safe, isolated, and fairly boring spot (separate child from the situation and people involved).
- Hold child firmly until over. (Don't use this if the tantrum turns into a physical struggle with you.)
- For an older child who loses her temper and has a fit, send her to her room or a "calm-down" spot to sit until she regains control of herself and stops "disturbing the peace."

Other Thoughts:
- Many parents and experts advise ignoring a tantrum, as long as no one is in danger of being hurt. Ignoring a

problem behavior deprives the child of an audience and any reward the attention might bring. This is difficult to do, however. Be aware the tantrum will usually intensify before diminishing.

■ The calmer *you* can be, the more quickly your child will calm down.

■ Do not respond by solving the problem that caused the child to tantrum. That just teaches her to throw a fit to get problems solved.

■ Do not spank—it only escalates a tantrum.

See also: Discussion of tantrums on page 51

TATTLES

Level of Offensiveness: 1 = Annoying

Natural Consequences:
- Damage to relationships.

Logical Consequence Possibilities:
- Look the child straight in the eye and ask, "What do you want me to do about it?" If your child is trying to get someone else into trouble, he will likely slink away.
- Parent refuses to help when there's tattling. Say, "I don't solve problems you can solve for yourself. Go work it out with your brother." Then ignore. Or, ask, "Is anything broken? Is there blood?" If the answers are No, then tell your child he needs to solve the problem himself.
- One warning and then a brief removal from the activity for each tattling episode.

Other Thoughts:
- Children tattle for a variety of reasons: they want to see someone else get in trouble, look good in comparison, get attention, or have the adult solve the problem for them. I recommend logical consequences only for the repeat tattling offender. Most young children need to be taught the difference between tattling and telling and then develop their own problem-solving skills.*
- Dismiss the problem by saying, "Well, I'm glad *you* know the rule," and then turn away.

See also: Blames others

---

*See Kathryn Hammerseng's useful little children's book on tattling: *Telling Isn't Tattling*, (Seattle, WA: Parenting Press, 1995).

THROWS THINGS WHEN ANGRY

Level of Offensiveness: 2 = Important to Address

Natural Consequences:
- Items may be broken.
- People can get hurt.

Logical Consequence Possibilities:
- If something is broken as a result, child must pay to have it repaired or replaced. (If this is a recurring problem, then sell a toy to pay for the broken item.)
- Child must pick up item thrown, put it away, and then go to room.
- Take away object thrown (especially if it belongs to the child) for the rest of the day (or one hour for a very young child).

Other Thoughts:
- Teach your young child that only certain items and areas are for throwing. Explain that people and things can get hurt.
- Make sure that you do not allow casual throwing in the house (sports balls, balled-up socks, etc.) that could escalate.
- Work with your child on appropriate ways to express anger.*

See also: Damages property

---

*See Elizabeth Crary's helpful books for children on anger management: *I'm Mad* and *I'm Furious* (Seattle, WA: Parenting Press, Inc., 1992 and 1994). For ages 1-3, see my board book, co-authored with Elizabeth Crary, *When You're Mad and You Know It*, (Seattle, WA: Parenting Press, Inc., 1996).

WON'T PICK UP TOYS

Level of Offensiveness: 1 = Annoying

Natural Consequences:
- Can't find the toys he wants.
- Toys get broken or pieces get lost.

Logical Consequence Possibilities:
- If child complains of being too tired to pick up, send him to bed until he is "rested." Do not allow any playing or reading in bed. As soon as he gets up, he is required to pick up his toys.
- If the bedroom floor is strewn with toys, say, "It isn't safe to walk in here, so Daddy and I can't come in to read you a bedtime story."
- Say, "If you're not willing to be responsible for your toys, you will not be able to play with any until the ones on the floor are picked up."
- Say, "We have such a mess in your room that it isn't safe. No friends can come over until it's picked up."
- Loss of the activity that made the mess (craft, playing with toys, cooking). Say, "People who don't help clean up, don't get to do these fun things." The next time you do it, give that child a solitary activity to do.
- If your pick-up time is at the end of the day, child must pick up three toys or he goes straight to bed without a story. If he dawdles, he misses the beginning of the bedtime story (go ahead and start without him).
- Toys not picked up get put out of reach by parent. Child must pay a fine (from allowance) to recover each toy.
- Say, "If you don't do your part in clean-up, I will assign you one of my jobs, too."
- The toys left on the floor get put away for a day or two.

■ No discretionary activities (or snacks) until all toys are picked up.
■ Child must sit in a boring spot until he's ready to pick up toys.

Other Thoughts:
■ A reward chart works well at motivating children to pick up toys. Wean them off the system by lengthening it: start with one day, then one week, then three weeks.
■ Break the task down into smaller, more manageable pieces. For example, say, "First, pick up all the dinosaurs. Now pick up the crayons. Now the stuffed animals." Stay with the child and supervise, but don't help him.
■ Make pick up into a game. Sing a clean-up song as you work. (The Barney™ clean-up song works well.) Or have the child choose a color and then pick up all the blue toys. Then do the other colors till all toys are put away.
■ Make sure children know where the toys go. Designate certain shelves or boxes for different types of toys. Label them with pictures for pre-readers.
■ Do you have too many toys out and making clutter? Try putting some away and rotating toys every two weeks or so.
■ Take a good look at how you keep your own room. Make sure you're practicing what you preach.

See also: Won't clean room

ABUSES VOLUME CONTROL ("But Mom! I can't hear it at all!")

Level of Offensiveness: 2 = Important to Address

Natural Consequences:
- Possible damage to hearing.

Logical Consequence Possibilities:
- Most TVs have a volume control that appears on the screen like this: lllllllllllll. Tape a bright yellow arrow under the screen (not interfering with the picture) to show the children where the limit is. If you check the volume and find it above the yellow arrow, the TV goes off. Make a habit of checking so the kids are less likely to test you. Establish limits for cd/tape players and radios as well.
- Politely request child turn it down. If child ignores you or it goes up again, say, "You can turn it down or turn it off for the rest of the day." Follow through immediately.

Other Thoughts:
- Some parents find it useful to get earphones for their children. If you do this, make sure the volume they select will not harm their hearing.
- Make sure you are not abusing the volume control yourself (or after your children are in bed). If you require Sesame Street® to be played at a low level, but have Star Trek® cranked up high, you are not treating your children respectfully, and they will probably follow suit.

WHINES

Level of Offensiveness: 1 = Annoying

Natural Consequences:
- People stop listening or wanting to be around child.

Logical Consequence Possibilities:
- Say, "That voice hurts my ears. You'll have to use that voice in your room where I can't hear it." Send her to her room.
- Child automatically does not get what she's whining for. Or, say, "I can't understand you when you whine" and ignore until she uses a regular voice.
- Parent doesn't give child any attention (no holding or talking) until the whining stops.
- If you're in the car, stop in a safe spot and put the child out of the car until she's done whining. (Stay with her, but don't pay any attention to her.)
- Time-out.

Other Thoughts:
- Make sure your child knows what whining is. Model for her what a pleasant voice and a whiny voice sound like. Tell her clearly to use a pleasant voice.
- Think about the cause of the whining. If you've been running errands all afternoon and hauled your child along with you, expect some whining due to tiredness or hunger. Evaluate your expectations for your children and plan more realistically.
- When children are tired or hungry, they don't always realize they're whining. Give them a second chance. Say, "Start over using a nice voice" or "Are you sure you want to use that voice?"

■ Remind the child, "That sound is whining. I don't listen to whining. Come get me when you can use a good voice (big-girl/big-boy voice)," and walk away.

■ Set a rule: Whining gets you nothing.

■ Check your own voice tones. Many parents plead with their children in a whiny tone and model this behavior. It can be fun to set up a "Whining bank." Anyone caught whining has to contribute a set amount to the bank. Use the money for some fun family event.

LEAVES YARD OR HOUSE WITHOUT PERMISSION

Level of Offensiveness: 3 = Unsafe

Natural Consequences:
▪ Child could get hurt or lost.

Logical Consequence Possibilities:
▪ Say, "I guess I can't trust you not to leave. You'll have to stay within my eyesight for the rest of the day." (Choose boring tasks and errands to do for the afternoon.)
▪ Loss of going to [wherever child went] for three days.
▪ Parent immediately retrieves child. Grounded to the house for the next full day.
▪ Restriction to the house or yard (first offense = one day, second offense = two days, third offense = one week)
▪ Loss of going to next place child requests.

Other Thoughts:
▪ Having a child wander off can be very frightening. Explain to your children the reasons why parents must *always* know where they are. Model the behavior you want by courteously letting your children know where you are, if and where they can reach you, and when you will be back.
▪ Make sure you have clearly communicated to your child your rules and the boundaries of where she can go.

6
PLANNING FOR A SPECIFIC PROBLEM

You've read about consequences, looked through the many possibilities for good, learning-oriented ones, and read about how to deliver and enforce them. It's time to make a plan for a recurring behavior problem in your home. Below is a simple list of questions and directions that will get you started on making a plan.

Describe the misbehavior. When does it happen? Who is involved?

What do you want your child to do differently? (Be specific. It's not enough to say, "I want him to be nice." Be clear about what specific behaviors you want to see—for example, "I want him to use problem-solving skills to negotiate toy conflicts with his brother" or "I want him to use words, not his fists, to express his anger."

Which parenting techniques have you tried so far to solve this problem? (Include any natural consequences here.)

Which techniques could you try before using a consequence?

Brainstorm a list of 3-6 logical consequences you might use to solve the problem. Star the top three you think are most workable and you would be willing to actually use.

Make your plan.

EXAMPLE WORKSHEET

Describe the misbehavior. When does it happen? Who is involved?

Sierra, age seven, wants us to do things for her she can do herself, like choosing clothes and getting ready for school in the morning. She dawdles, whines, and complains that she can't find things, or that she can't do it herself. It's most annoying to me in the morning when I'm trying to get everyone out the door.

What do you want your child to do differently?

I want her to choose her clothes, get dressed, eat breakfast, and gather her school things and lunch, without help from me, by 8:30am.

Which parenting techniques have you tried so far to solve this problem?

Nagging. Yelling. I rescue her by remembering her lunch and backpack. I haven't let her experience any natural consequences yet.

Which techniques could you try before using a consequence?

- I could make up a chart for her of morning tasks to remind her of what needs to be done.
- I could require her to make her lunch and lay out her next day's outfit the night before.
- I could give her a lot of practice with choices so that she's more comfortable with and used to decision-making.

- I could reward her for successful mornings with a special treat in the afternoon.
- I could let her go without lunch if she forgets to bring it to school.
- I could make her a special, laminated Decision ticket. She gives it up once a day to have her dad or me make a decision for her. After that, she must make all her own decisions. If she still has it at the end of the day, one of us will read with her before bedtime.

Brainstorm a list of 3-6 logical consequences you might use to solve the problem.

- Loss of afternoon privileges like TV, snacks, friends.
- Give her a job of mine to do in the afternoon, since she took up my time in the morning doing her jobs.
- If she whines in the morning, I could ignore her, or say, "Sorry, my ears don't hear whining."
- If she doesn't have her lunch made by 8:15am, she goes without lunch, or just takes a packet of crackers and cheese with her.

Make your plan.

Since I value decision-making skills, I will work on giving Sierra lots of simple choices throughout the day to get her more comfortable with the process. I will have her choose her next day's outfit the night before and lay it out. If she doesn't have it chosen before her bedtime, she won't get a story that night. I will stop bringing her lunch to school. If these measures don't work to improve our mornings, I will give her an unpleasant job to do in the afternoon (she hates putting away her little brother's toys) to make up for wasting my time in the morning.

WORKSHEET

Describe the misbehavior.   When does it happen? Who is involved?

_____

_____

_____

_____

_____

_____

What do you want your child to do differently?

_____

_____

_____

Which parenting techniques have you tried so far to solve this problem?

_____

_____

_____

Which techniques could you try before using a consequence?

_____

_____

_____

_____

_____

_____

_____

Brainstorm a list of 3-6 logical consequences you might use to solve the problem.

_____

_____

_____

_____

_____

_____

_____

_____

_____

_____

_____

_____

Make your plan.

_____

_____

_____

_____

_____

_____

_____

_____

_____

_____

_____

_____

_____

CLOSING THOUGHTS

Parenting demands time and attention. Parenting by impulse or by your emotion of the moment can result in some pretty terrible scenes with your kids or regrets down the road. Respect the important job you're doing by giving it the thought it deserves. Your child's growth and maturity is directly affected by your thoughtful involvement. You can and do make such a difference.

Take heart in the fact that however many times you feel you've blown it, there are always more opportunities to guide and teach on the horizon. All honest efforts in parenting make some impact. Build on the good work you've already done and learn from what doesn't work. It is my hope that this book provides you with some good, workable ideas for consequences that teach and inspires you to use them well.

Books for Parents

Clarke, Jean Illsley. *Self-Esteem: A Family Affair.* New York: Harper & Row, 1978. Information on Being and Doing affirmations—and a lot more.

Clarke, Jean Illsley, *Time-In: When Time-Out Doesn't Work,* Seattle, WA: Parenting Press, 1999. Very good little book on helping parents to use discipline in a way that teaches the child how to do better.

Crary, Elizabeth. *Help! The Kids Are At It Again: Using Kids' Quarrels to Teach People Skills,* Seattle, WA: Parenting Press, Inc., 1997. I highly recommend this book for insight on why your kids aren't getting along and what to do about it.

Crary, Elizabeth. *Kids Can Cooperate: A Practical Guide to Teaching Problem Solving,* Seattle, WA: Parenting Press, Inc., 1984. A step-by-step guide to teaching children to negotiate conflicts—it's not hard to teach and such a powerful skill to give your kids.

Crary, Elizabeth. *Pick Up Your Socks...And Other Skills Growing Children Need,* Seattle, WA: Parenting Press, Inc., 1990. Lots of good, practical information on teaching your school-age children to be responsible for chores and homework. I love the chart on page 51.

Eyre, Linda & Richard. *Teaching Children Values,* New York: Simon & Schuster, 1993. Great book—one of the few out on this topic that actually gives you guidance on *how* to do it.

Eyre, Linda & Richard. *Three Steps to a Strong Family,* New York: Simon & Schuster, 1994. The Eyres offer very practical how-to information on raising responsible, caring children.

Faull, Jan. *Mommy! I Have to Go Potty!* Hemet, CA: Raefield-Roberts, Pub., 1996. If you're facing potty training or are having trouble with it, this is *the* book to have.

Faull, Jan. *Unplugging Power Struggles,* Seattle, WA: Parenting Press, 2000. Thoughtful and realistic options on how to end power struggles with your child.

Frankel, Fred. *Good Friends Are Hard to Find,* Pasadena, CA: Perspective Publishing, 1996. Very practical help for a variety of "friend" or peer issues: child has none, child has the wrong kind, poor sportsmanship, bullies, and more.

Huntley, Rebecca. *The Sleep Book for Tired Parents* by Seattle, WA: Parenting Press, Inc., 1991. Real help for a variety of sleep problems—I've lost track of how many times I've recommended this book.

Jones, James. *Let's Fix the Kids!* Westminister, CA: Familyhood, Inc., 1997. A set of tapes and accompanying manual help you set many parenting problems to rights.

Lickona, Thomas. *Raising Good Children: Helping Your Child Through the Stages of Moral Development,* New York: Bantam Books, 1983. This book really helps you understand how your everyday parenting affects your child's moral development—excellent book.

MacKenzie, Robert. *Setting Limits: How to Raise Responsible, Independent Children by Providing CLEAR Boundaries,* rev. ed., Rocklin, CA: Prima Publishing, 1998. Terrific information on rules and limits and lots of help for homework problems.

Nelson, Jane. *Positive Discipline,* rev. ed., New York: Ballantine Books, 1996. Helpful for distinguishing between discipline and punishment.

Neville, Helen & Clark, Diane Johnson. *Temperament Tools,* Seattle, WA: Parenting Press, 1998. Very practical, day-to-day help with different temperament types—particularly useful with young children.

Ricker, Audrey & Crowder, Carolyn. *Backtalk: Four Steps to Ending Rude Behavior in Your Kids,* New York: Simon & Schuster, 1998. If there's an on-going problem with backtalk in your home, go get this book. It will help.

Rosemond, John. *John Rosemond's Six-Point Plan for Raising Happy, Healthy Children,* Kansas City, MO: Andrews & McNeel, 1989. A back-to-basics type of approach to parenting.

Rosemond, John. *Parent Power! A Common Sense Approach to Parenting in the 90's and Beyond,* 2nd ed., Kansas City, MO: Andrews & McNeel, 1990. Covers a variety of misbehaviors.

Shick, Lyndall. *Understanding Temperament,* Seattle, WA: Parenting Press, Inc., 1998. Useful for understanding how different temperaments in a family contribute to harmony or discord.

Straus, Murray A. *Ten Myths About Spanking Children,* Durham, NH: Family Research Laboratory, University of New Hampshire, 1992. This is a summary report based on Straus' study on how spanking affects children in a long-term way.

Tracy, Louise Felton. *Grounded for Life?! Stop Blowing Your Fuse and Start Communicating With Your Teenager,* Seattle, WA: Parenting Press, Inc., 1994. Really great information on day-to-day issues of misbehavior and responsibility with teens.

Books for Parents to Read with Their Children

Anderson, Peggy King. *First Day Blues*. Parenting Press, Inc., Seattle, WA: 1992. A choose-your-own-ending story on making friends at a new school. Ages 7-11.

Bosch, Carl W. *Bully on the Bus*. Parenting Press, Inc., Seattle, WA: 1988. A choose-your-own-ending story about being bullied. Great ideas. Ages 7-11.

Bosch, Carl W. *Making the Grade*. Parenting Press, Inc., Seattle, WA: 1991. A choose-your-own-ending story about getting a bad report card and what to do about it. Ages 7-11.

Crary, Elizabeth. *Finders, Keepers*. Parenting Press, Inc., Seattle, WA: 1987. A choose-your-own-ending story about honesty and stealing. Ages 7-11.

Crary, Elizabeth. The Children's Problem Solving series: *I Want It, I Can't Wait, I Want to Play, My Name Is Not Dummy, I'm Lost*, Seattle, WA: Parenting Press, 1996. A fun and easy way to introduce problem solving. Useful with ages 3 to 8.

Crary, Elizabeth. Dealing with Feelings series: *I'm Mad, I'm Frustrated, I'm Proud*, Seattle, WA: Parenting Press, Inc., 1992, and *I'm Furious, I'm Scared, I'm Excited*, Seattle, WA: Parenting Press, Inc., 1994. Helpful for getting children to think about their options for expressing strong emotions. Useful with ages 3 to 9.

Crary, Elizabeth & Steelsmith, Shari. The Feelings for Little Children series: *When You're Mad and You Know It, When You're Happy and You Know It, When You're Shy and You Know It, When You're Silly and You Know It*. Seattle, WA: Parenting Press, Inc., 1996. Really fun way to introduce feeling words and ways to express them with the young set—you can even sing the text! These board books are useful with ages 1 to 3.

Hammerseng, Kathryn. *Telling Isn't Tattling*, Seattle, WA: Parenting Press, 1995. A great way to start talking about a tough subject: when is it telling and when is it tattling? Useful with ages 4 to 12.

Laik, Judy. *Under Whose Influence?* Seattle, WA: Parenting Press, Inc. 1994. A choose-your-own-ending story about the choice to drink alcohol or not. Ages 7-11.

About the Author

Shari Steelsmith and her husband are the parents of three children, ages 10, 6, and 2. They live, work, and occasionally struggle with various misbehaviors near the San Jacinto mountains of southern California.

Shari is a full-time mother and a freelance writer focusing on parenting, educational, and family-related topics. She writes the weekly parenting *Tip & Tool* articles for the website ParentingPress.com.

She is also the author of:

- *Peekaboo: And Other Games to Play With Your Baby* (Parenting Press, Inc.),
- *How to Open & Operate a Home-Based Daycare Business* (Globe Pequot Press),
- The Feelings for Little Children series—
  When You're Happy and You Know It,
  When You're Mad and You Know It,
  When You're Shy and You Know It, and
  When You're Silly and You Know It (Parenting Press, Inc.),

as well as two biographies for young children. She is currently working on a book about children's anger and parents' options.

steals, 132-33
strokes. *See* being and doing
    affirmations

T

table, won't stay at, 134
takes things without permission,
    135
tantrums, 51, 136-37
tattles, 138
teases, unkindly. *See* sibling,
    mistreats
teeth, won't brush, 44, 120-22
throws things, 140
toilet training, problems, 45, 122
toys, won't pick up, 44, 111-13,
    140-41

V

volume control, abuses, 142

W

warnings, 20
whines, 143-44

Y

yard, leaves without
    permission, 145

ORDER FORM

___ **Mommy! I Have to Go Potty! – $13.95**
A simple, common-sense approach to teaching your toddler to use the toilet. This clear, step-by-step method will take your child all the way from diapers to dry nights. 130 pages

___ **Go To Your Room! Consequences That Teach – $14.95**
Many, many ideas for using consequences that teach. 160 pages

Feelings for Little Children Series – $5.95 each
Colorful, fun board books in rhyming text helps toddlers learn the words for four feelings and offers them healthy ways to express these common emotions.
___ **When You're Happy and You Know It,** 10 pages
___ **When You're Mad and You Know It,** 10 pages
___ **When You're Silly and You Know It,** 10 pages
___ **When You're Shy and You Know It,** 10 pages

Tools for Everyday Parenting Series – $9.95 each
Great books for new parents. They present information in both text and cartoon illustrations. Each practical book offers tried-and-true suggestions and tools for improving parenting skills.
___ **Magic Tools for Raising Kids,** 128 pages
___ **365 Wacky, Wonderful Ways to Get Your Children to Do What You Want,** 104 pages
___ **Peekaboo & Other Games to Play with Your Baby,** 120 pages
___ **Joyful Play with Toddlers,** 128 pages
___ **Taking Care of Me,** 112 pages

Available at bookstores or call toll-free **1-800-992-6657** (Visa & MasterCard accepted). When ordering by mail, please add $5.00 (for orders totalling $1-$20) or $6.00 (for orders of $21-$50) for shipping via UPS. WA residents add 8.6% sales tax.

Name _____

Address _____

_____

Phone: _____

Send Order to: Parenting Press, Dept. 205, P.O. Box 75267, Seattle, WA 98125. In Canada, call Raincoast Book Dist., 1-800-663-5714. Prices subject to change without notice.